Who Needs a Lutheran College?

VALUES VISION VOCATION

Tom Christenson

Lutheran University Press
Minneapolis, Minnesota

Who Needs a Lutheran College?
by Tom Christenson

Library of Congress Cataloging-in-Publication Data
Christenson, Tom.
  Who needs a Lutheran college/university? / Thomas Christenson.
    p. cm.
  Includes bibliographical references.
  ISBN-13: 978-1-932688-57-3 (alk. paper)
  ISBN-10: 1-932688-57-9 (alk. paper)
 1. Lutheran universities and colleges--United States. 2. Education, Humanistic--United States. 3. Education, Higher--Aims and objectives--United States. I. Title.
  LC574.C48 2011
  378.071'4173--dc22

                              2010049581

Cover photos courtesy of Augsburg College, Concordia College, and Lutheran Theological Seminary at Gettysburg. Used with permission.

Lutheran University Press, PO Box 390759, Minneapolis, MN 55439
Manufactured in the United States of America

Table of Contents

A Few Notes About These Essays

Academic year 2002-2003 saw the publication of *The Gift and Task of Lutheran Higher Education*, my first book on Lutheran higher education. Since its publication, I have been asked to the campuses of over half of the Evangelical Lutheran Church in America (ELCA) colleges and universities and a small number of Lutheran Church—Missouri Synod (LCMS) colleges. I have also been the guest of Lutheran Education Australia where I had the opportunity to address teachers and other education leaders in the rapidly growing Lutheran school system there. These essays usually began as talks prepared for those visits. But very often they were also prompted by conversations I had with faculty, students, college presidents, and trustees of these institutions. These many visits have certainly been and continue to be learning occasions for me.

These essays are short. When they were addresses they were almost always longer, combining more than one focal issue or including explanatory sections that I have since edited out because I did not want to repeat the same things over and over again. In spite of that editing, the reader will notice that the issues raised and the arguments made overlap each other. It is, I believe, in the nature of the subject that they should revisit many of the same themes. Some of these essays initially addressed concerns encountered at a particular institution. I guess I should not have been surprised to find that they ended up being relevant far beyond my expectations. For example, when I wrote *Gift and Task,* it never occurred to me that what I wrote there would be relevant to education in Australia, nor that the peculiar issues that concerned the Australian educators would be so relevant to colleges and universities here in the States. It was not initially apparent to me that discussions I had at ELCA colleges would be on target for LCMS schools. But that has, again and again, turned out to be the case.

I have edited these essays into a single volume at the encouragement of many people at the schools who formed their initial audiences. Many who had read the earlier book noted that my thinking had evolved since its publication and that it was time to put these new thoughts into print. There is nothing that I write now that is inconsistent with what I wrote then, but I do believe my thinking now has a slightly different focus. Certain issues that were then on the periphery of my thinking are now central and vice-versa. I use the terms "college" and "university" pretty much inter-changeably. Sometimes I use both. I will sometimes use just one term throughout an essay, but it is not my intention to exclude the other, just to avoid repeating both terms continuously.

These essays are arranged in three groupings. Chapters One and Two are about asking and focusing the title question. Chapters Three through Seven are about answering it. The remaining sections are about the implications of the answer I offer and some specific applications. If impatient readers want to get to the heart of the argument, they would do well to go immediately to Chapters Five and Seven.

I am encouraged by the continuing lively interest in Lutheran higher education. The serious reconsideration of what being a Lutheran college means is a good sign that the species is alive. The number of forums on this topic is growing as is the number of campuses that have established something like a center for faith and learning to keep the conversation going. The small part I have been able to play in this process has been a real pleasure for me. I hope it has also been useful to others.

As a consequence of the fact that many of these essays sprang up in dialogue, many of the ideas herein are the work of other people. For example, Chapter Eight on Educating the Whole Person and Chapter Eleven on Shaping the Culture of a College were written in response to retreats for Capital University faculty and administration. I take responsibility for the ideas presented there, but I certainly was not the sole source of them. It is to the faculty and administration of my own and other colleges who participated in such discussions that I dedicate this volume.

Tom Christenson
Summer 2010

CHAPTER ONE

Who Needs a Lutheran College/University? Taking the Question Seriously

This is not a rhetorical question. The number of college-age young people is diminishing across the country. In some areas those decreases are more dramatic than in others. Yet in almost every state the question is being seriously asked, "How many tertiary institutions will be required?" Following that question is this: "What kind of institutions do these need to be?" So, if we begin with the premise that not all the colleges in the U.S. will survive—particularly private colleges—we then have to seriously pose the question, "Who needs a Lutheran college/university?"

The answer to this question will depend on:

What we perceive the real educational needs of students and the world to be.

What we perceive the essential identity of Lutheran colleges and universities to be.

What do Lutheran colleges/universities have to offer that cannot be just as well (and more cheaply?) delivered by other institutions.

In nature there are two basic survival techniques for animals in a hostile environment. One is to be the swiftest, strongest, healthiest members of the herd or pack. The second is to blend in, to stay invisible somewhere in the middle, to do nothing to call attention to oneself. Humans (and human institutions) are tempted to behave in the same ways. The larger, stronger ones with most endurance are not afraid to be seen and noticed for what gives them strength. But those with less confidence are tempted to become invisible, becoming generic colleges/universities in the market place.

I do not know how many times I have heard someone say something like this: "We don't want to say too loudly that we are a Lutheran university because it will offend prospective students (or their parents) and chase them away. Better to pretend that we are nothing special, that we offer generic degrees by means of generic courses offered by generic (and often out-sourced) faculty. If we have no identity, then no one will be scared away by it." Of course this reasoning contains questionable assumptions and commits a huge fallacy. But that has never prevented a view from being popularly espoused, so . . .

I firmly believe that the worst thing we (Lutheran colleges/universities) can do is try to be generic institutions. We will be under-sold by the Walmarts of the academic world who will sell the same generic merchandise at a much lower price. The next to the worst thing we can do is to offer something that is unique and truly valuable but not tell anyone (even ourselves) about it for fear of "offending someone." The third worst thing we can do is to avoid thinking about it in the hope that the whole thing will go away and we will survive just because of market momentum.

On the assumption that I am right about this, I once again invite you to think through the basic questions: What does it mean to be a Lutheran college/university? Of what treasure that students and the world needs are we the stewards? Where will we get the freedom (and the courage) to be who we are at the same time we become who we can be?

CHAPTER TWO

What Does It Mean To Be a Lutheran College? Why Are We Still Asking?

I have lost track of how many discussions I have been part of that focus on the question, "What does it mean to be a Lutheran college/ university?" The question may be framed differently on different occasions, but it seems to be the essential question because it comes up over and over again. Eventually someone in the discussion will say, "But we talked about this just three years ago. Why do we keep coming back to this again and again? Why are we still asking after all these years?"

Here are a few answers I have developed:

1. The question needs revisiting because people continue to misunderstand what the possible answers might be. Our minds are largely shaped by our culture, and it is very difficult to think outside the boxes the culture provides us. When we think of religiously-affiliated education, we often assume that it will be parochial, narrow, doctrinaire, and bent on making converts, and that it will want to teach its own views and silence all others. If religious education is not like that, then, the supposition runs, it must not be really religious. That is, either the college/university is parochial, narrow, doctrinaire, etc., or it is not really a religiously-affiliated institution. If the school took its religious character seriously, it would end up re-establishing the Inquisition. It is not doing the latter, so it must not be doing the former. It does not seem to matter how often that view is corrected, people's minds snap back to it like a rubber band.

Because that false either/or seems perennially to shape our thinking, it needs a perennial corrective—or at least one that occurs regularly. When people begin to remember that Lutheran higher education intentionally avoids the either/or boxes the culture provides, the necessity of revisiting the "What is a Lutheran college/university?"

question may diminish. Until then we ask the question because we are not happy with the alternative answers the culture offers us.

2. The question about Lutheran higher education may be asked very generally, but it needs to be lived out very particularly. Individual colleges/universities need to ask the question, "What does it mean for *this* college that it is Lutheran?"

In other sections I will talk about the vocational model of Lutheran higher education. For now let me just say that I think of vocation as the intersection of gifts and needs. So our vocation as an institution is manifest where the world's needs and our own gifts intersect. The vocation of one university may not be the same as another one. One may be located in the heart of a large urban area. Another may be located in a small town in rural America. The environs for education bring with them both different needs and different gifts. It would be a mistake if these two institutions were identical or tried to be.

The same institution may change over time. The needs of the students an institution serves may change over a twenty-year period. The needs of the world they will go on to serve after they graduate will change as well. The programs that were strong and focal may no longer be; the faculty who brought life to a particular program or generation may now be retired. So the question, "What is our vocation?" may well have a different answer now than it had a generation ago. The question needs to be asked once again.

3. I remember a discussion where someone said, "It's a characteristic of a Lutheran college that it's a place that keeps on asking, 'What does it mean to be a Lutheran college?'"

Lutherans have, from the very beginning, been question raisers. Luther's *Theses* for debate sparked a rethinking. His *Heidelberg Disputation* pressed the issue further. Luther's *Small Catechism* continually raises the question, "What does this mean?" The idea that is clearly conveyed is that the serious asking of questions is appropriate, even essential, as is the learning of answers.

4. A sincere question is an invitation to speak and a promise to listen. A community focused by a set of questions has at its heart an intentional regard of the other and an openness about it. That regard and openness does not need to be discussed if it is obviously shown

by the community of discourse. How willing am I to hear a brand new answer? How willing are we to risk a new way of looking at things? If we are not willing, then we had better not invite a new response, we had better not open with a question.

A sincere question is also an expression of a willingness to learn. I take the fact that we ask and rethink the question so seriously and so often as a sign of health. It is more a sign of health, I would argue, than having on hand a too-ready answer. Such an answer can become a pious platitude. It can also be a way of avoiding the probing and re-velatory character of the question.

Way back at the beginning of my teaching career, I served as a substitute art teacher in elementary schools in Connecticut. One of the principals I worked for one day gave me a powerful piece of advice: "Every time you walk into the classroom take a few moments to ask yourself the question, 'What am I trying to do here?' If you fail to do that you will simply end up doing to your students what your worst teachers did to you. Teachers, on the other hand, who daily ask that mind-opening question stay alive to teaching. For them it is a creative and growing experience."

Asking again, "What is a Lutheran college/university?" is a way of re-asking, as that principal put it, "What are we trying to do here?" I'm very happy whenever I see that this question is alive and posed with some seriousness.

CHAPTER THREE

The Christian Calling in Education

There are several reasons why Christians have a calling in education. Some of them are fairly obvious, others may be not as obvious.

- Jesus was a teacher. His disciples certainly confirmed this was so since they referred to him by that title. Those who gathered around him noticed this and asked, on occasion, why he taught by telling stories, for which he had become noted. This means that those who gathered around him were learners, and the whole community of them had an educational focus.

- When people came to write about Jesus they showed him teaching and they showed those who heard him either catching his message or missing it. But more than being the record of Jesus' teaching, the gospels themselves have a teaching focus and function. The gospels relate parables, but in many respects they are also parable-like. A kind of teaching is taking place there in the story that is told and in the way it is told. There is definitely something of great value to be learned by seriously engaging such a text.

- The community that Jesus gathered had a teaching function for they showed, through the way they treated each other, something about the presence of God's kingdom in their midst. This witness continued in the community beyond Jesus's departure, explained as a "gift of the Spirit."

We need to take a little journey of the imagination and move ourselves back to the first centuries of the Christian era. We are in the Roman empire, a world where the political, economic, and military agendas are all set by Rome. In the midst of this empire there is a small enclave of people who call themselves Christians, followers of a crucified Nazarene peasant named Jesus whom these followers see as the anointed one of God, the Christ.

The empire abounds with religious movements and cults of every imaginable sort, but what makes these Christians interesting is not the believability of their stories or the beauty of their liturgy, but how they come together as a community. The distinctions that play such an absolute role in the normal world (whether one is free or slave, Roman or barbarian, wealthy or poor, insider or outsider, well or diseased, male or female, law maker or law breaker, righteous or sinner) do not matter to the Christians. All that counts for status in the Roman world counts for nothing in their midst. People who come here are invited to leave those old identities behind, to become new people in Christ, unified in his Spirit. Some of the most disreputable people gather here—prostitutes, tax collectors, slaves, slave owners, lepers, Roman toadies. I can imagine respectable people responding, "There goes the neighborhood!" When the Christians are gathered, it is like a recovery group, a start-over group, a new life group. They are radically egalitarian, radically pacifist, radically communitarian, radically welcoming, radically caring, radically thankful, and radically forgiving. It is a rather scary concept, but that is what makes them interesting.

Christians were, from the beginning, a group with a difference. They did not buy into the dominant culture's concepts of power, human worth, or status. They did not think in terms of society's insiders and outsiders. They understood what it was to fear, love, and worship differently. That difference from the dominant culture is what made their contemporaries take note of them, in many cases fear and despise them, and in some cases join them. The church was an identifiable community because of the way they lived, because of the things they did and did not value, and because of the provocative way they thought about the world. Those Christians were culture-critical from the outset, and, I think, if there are any of them left, they still would be.

Now, the question I would have us ask is: Does this community of Christians have an educational mission? The answer should be *so* obvious: Yes! More than that, this community *is* an educational mission.

The second question we should ponder is: Does such a community in any way resemble what we today call the church? Has the church lost sight of its educational mission because it has largely lost site of what a radical reality it is? Or has it become, as Wendell Berry says, a society "exclusively dedicated to incanting anemic souls into heaven"?

Being Lutheran, we see that any statement of what the church is must tell the sinner *and* saint story. The church today is salt that has pretty much lost its savor. It is a chameleon community that blends so well into the background of middle class America as to have become invisible. Christians do, more often than not, worship the whole pantheon of gods that the empire recognizes—success, power, prestige, comfort, respectability, entertainment, and oblivion. But at the same time the church is still a community:

> sharing, celebrating, and stewarding giftedness
>
> oriented to the paradigmatic figure of Jesus, the crucified one
>
> challenging the grip of the dominant paradigms of power, wealth, control
>
> suspicious and critical of all the world's claims to ultimacy
>
> naming the sources of illusion, alienation, and fear
>
> responding to the deep needs of others
>
> realizing a love that leads beyond preoccupation with self
>
> engaged in realizing God's reign in the present world

If this is not a community with an educational mission, then what community is? Such a community will be a place of serious discussion; a place of liberation; a place for the transforming of persons; a place for the imagining of new worlds; a place for learning, hard thinking, earnest debate, faithful criticism, and the sharing of such learning; and a place for thanksgiving and celebration.

Christians have a mission for education because they have always been about teaching and learning. Christians have a mission in education because they have so much to offer that the world so desperately needs. Christians have a mission in education because it is a natural expression of what it means to be Christian in the world.

CHAPTER FOUR

The Lutheran Calling in Education

As well as the Christian calling in education there is also a particularly Lutheran calling that flavors colleges and universities that stand in the Lutheran tradition. Some parts of this "Lutheran difference" come out of Lutheran belief, but many of them also come out of the circumstances of Lutheran history and practice.

1. The Lutheran movement started in a university setting.

Lutherans, among Christians, have a different relation to the university than many denominations. If it were not for a bunch of faculty and students at the University of Wittenberg there would not be any Lutherans at all. It was their questioning, their calling for debate and open discussion, their re-interpretation of Scripture and tradition that planted the seeds of reformation. Luther's 95 Theses were an assignment for his students before they were a public call for debate and, ultimately, for reform.

My own favorite definition of a teacher is a communicative learner. Luther certainly embodied that. It was as a teacher preparing his lectures that Luther considered again the message of the Scriptures. It was in that process of re-reading that Luther discovered a new God, not the fiercely distant judge whom humans must try desperately to reach, but the gift-giving God who comes with open arms to us. Rather than seeing religiousness as our effort to build a bridge to God, he saw religiousness as our celebration that God has already crossed over. Had Luther not been an open-minded learner, he never would have been the teacher he was.

That story ought to be at the heart of the Lutheran church's identity, and it ought to be at the heart of the Lutheran university's identity. The relation between church and college ought not be a "howdy stranger" sort of relationship. A trip to a university campus ought to be, for contemporary Lutherans, more like a homecoming.

2. Luther embodied engaged and loving criticism.

The Lutheran church came to be out of an action of faithful criticism by Luther and other university faculty of the practices of the church. Lutherans have a call to be exemplars of faithful and loving criticism. We are familiar with skeptical criticism and cynical criticism—a criticism that doubts everything and commits itself to nothing. That is not what Luther practiced. His criticism was born out of love, concern, and faith—a faith bold enough to question and courageous enough to try to change what was wrong with the institution he loved.

Luther was critical of the church, but he was also critical of the rulers of his day, the education system, the system of banking. He was critical of other theologians, some of whom were quite good friends, and he was critical of himself. It is only appropriate, then, that Lutheran higher education should practice engaged criticism. We should learn to be critical of the culture and its assumptions; we should learn to be critical of our institutions and the ways we are tempted to make them serve their own needs rather than the needs of the society as a whole. We should be especially critical of those things that claim ultimate loyalty and those things that resist most violently being critiqued. We should learn to be self-critical, applying to ourselves at least the same standards that we expect of others.

Lutheran colleges and universities should be places where engaged criticism is practiced. It should be a place where students can witness and participate in a community of critical discourse, where the most difficult and important issues can be engaged and the most diverse views can be fairly heard and thoroughly examined.

3. Luther's conceptions of freedom and vocation.

These ideas, as much as any, shape the Lutheran understanding of education. They are essentially connected to Luther's understanding of God's grace, a redemption that we, as humans, do not deserve but that comes to us as a loving gift. Because of this gift, we are free from having to justify our place as God's children. Because of this gift, we are free to see and to serve the real need of our neighbor. How do we receive that gift? By passing it along. The image that comes to my mind is the crystal prism. Into one side comes the full-spectrum intense light of the sun. Out the other side is refracted the full rainbow of colors. We are like that prism; the love of God is the light that empowers the whole thing. Out the other side comes the refracted love of God to be shared for the needs of the world. Vocation, in Luther's view, is the calling to serve, in love, the deep needs of those we have at hand to serve. Parents do that in tending the needs of their children. Doctors and nurses do that in tending the needs of the sick. Farmers and fishermen do that in providing for our needs for food. Legislators and constables do that by serving our need for good laws and good order.

Can education be such a service? Doubly so, for it serves not only the immediate needs of students for learning, but it also serves the needs of the world that those students, through their vocations, will serve. For this reason Luther pressed the civic and religious leaders of his day for a commitment to education. Luther gives many reasons why the education of young men and women should be a priority, but foremost among them is for the long-term welfare of the community. Luther writes:

> It behooves the council and the authorities to devote the greatest care and attention to the education of the young. Since the property, honor and life of the whole city have been committed to their faithful keeping, they would be remiss in their duty if they did not seek its welfare and improvement with all the means at their command. . . . A city's best and greatest welfare, safety and strength consist in its having many able, learned, wise, honorable and well-educated citizens. . . . . Since a city should have educated people and since there is today a universal dearth of them and complaint that they are not to be found, we dare not wait until they spring up of themselves. . . . Nor will God produce miracles as long as men can solve their problems by means of the other gifts he has already granted.

Lutherans have a calling in education wherever there is a genuine need that we have some ability to serve. Does the world have a need for caring, concerned, critical, skilled, and learned people? Obviously, yes. It is in the educating of such persons that the calling of Lutheran colleges and universities is expressed.

4. Luther saw knowing as a kind of piety.

Luther said, "How dare you not know what can be known?" What Luther was expressing here is not, I think, an exclusively Christian view, but what I would call a proper biblical view. If the world is God's creation, then God's nature is lavishly revealed in it. How can we turn our backs on it in disinterest? Why should we not attend, like the psalmist, to the wonders that are being worked there? The seas, the clouds, the mountains, the sun, the moon, the stars, the plains and magnificent forests, and the creatures great and small are all the subjects of the psalmist's hymns of awe and thanksgiving.

The creation, like a gift, should be caringly unwrapped, not just because it contains something that may be of immediate use to us, but because of the wonder of the gift and the generosity of the giver. A careful, appreciative, wonder-filled knowing is an act of piety. A refusal to know, a turning of one's back on the creation, is more than laziness or poor stewardship, it is an act of blasphemy.

So much of our modern, Western way of viewing the world is utilitarian. It is almost as though we expect that children will lose their natural curiosity and sense of wonder. What kind of notion of maturation does our culture operate with if that is so? Yet we know that this loss of wonder is not a necessary outcome of aging. We may all know people—artists, great scientists, as well as quite ordinary folks who are still wonderers.

A Lutheran place of learning should be a place for the wonder to awaken, an asylum for those who cannot understand how someone would not be fascinated by geologic time, galactic clusters, the lives of whales and butterflies, the construction of the eyeball, the workings of a brain, the intricacy of an ecosystem or an economy.

5. Lutherans have practiced *paideutic* education.

At Capital University, where I teach, there is a sign that welcomes people to campus and that designates the campus as an historic landmark. Among other things that are written there is a quote from the university's mission statement, "Capital University — Transforming lives through education." That statement expresses what I have called the paideutic view of education, the view of education as *paideia*, that is, the development of persons.

We can easily get wrapped up in the view that education is mainly the learning of subjects, i.e. facts and skills, bits of information collected into digestible units. These things are certainly important. An orthopedist needs to know the bones in the foot, an historian needs to know events and persons and dates, a reader or speaker of German needs to know which prepositions take the dative. But if that were all that education provided, then education could be accomplished by purchasing a good encyclopedia. If one were to interview the alumni of Lutheran colleges and universities, I believe they would almost universally attest that another kind of learning happened to them in the process of learning these other things. While learning anatomy, history, or German grammar, they also came to be considerable human beings.

This occurs partly through the discipline of learning; partly through the study of the humanities; partly through the example of professors and peers; partly through playing on a team or singing in the choir; partly through being challenged to articulate and explain one's beliefs; and partly through service projects, community engagement, internships, etc. In many ways this dimension of learning has never been focal or intentional, but it always has been an essential part of the Lutheran college experience.

Where did I learn to value classical music? Where did I learn to appreciate visual art? Where did I learn to listen to poetry, to see the world through a variety of eyes? Where did I learn to read a text critically, to deeply engage the author in a dialogue that would change my understanding of myself and the world? Where did I learn to expect good arguments from others and from myself? Where did I learn that what one gets out of an encounter with a text of any kind is proportional to what one puts into it? Where did I learn that I must understand an author before I begin to criticize him/her? Where did I learn that humans have not always looked at the world in the same way, that the same word may have meant something very different, that meanings evolve? Where did I learn that people can delude themselves and live quite totally unaware of the harm they do to others? All of these things require an encounter, many of them also require the gaining of information or a skill. Many of them also require a change in attitude, a change in orientation, and a change in self. A college that does this has assisted in the creation of a human being. David Orr has written:

> The goal of education is not [merely] mastery of subject matter but mastery of one's person. Subject matter is simply the tool. Much as one would use a hammer and chisel to carve a block of marble, one uses ideas and knowledge

to forge ones own personhood. For the most part we labor under a confusion of ends and means, thinking that the goal of education is to stuff all kinds of facts, techniques, and information into students' minds regardless of how and with what effect it will be used.

It is not, of course, that only Lutheran colleges do such paideutic education. But every Lutheran college I have ever encountered does it. I cannot quote any line from Luther to demonstrate why that should be so. Somehow it must have been part of the fabric of Lutheran family or congregational life. Whatever its source, it is one of the gifts we bring to the educational enterprise.

6. Lutherans have come to embrace the wider world, to welcome and value diversity.

We cannot honestly claim that we have always done that. For a large part of our history, Lutheran colleges and universities were "for us, by us" institutions. Not that many decades ago Lutheran colleges had few, if any, non-Lutheran faculty. Those who were present were made to feel like definite outsiders in many respects.

For most of us that not only has changed, but it has changed radically. Institutions that once were cloisters in a hostile world have learned how to reach out and embrace their neighbors and neighborhoods. Colleges that were "safe havens" for young people now challenge them with global outlook and outreach. We have learned not just to tolerate people of other faith and cultural traditions but to value them. We are learning to see difference not as a problem but as a gift.

I do not believe that this change is an accident. I think there are good Lutheran reasons for moving in that direction. Let me mention just a few here:

- We are all adopted children of God, brought into the family by God's grace, not by any accomplishment or merit on our part. On what grounds would we justify an "us/them" way of looking at others?

- Called to serve the deep needs of the world and the real needs of our neighbors, we must encounter many views and voices to see what those needs are and address them helpfully. We do not believe we are sanctified into wisdom. The voice of the other is necessary for hard truth to be told and heard.

- Lutherans have always been critical and self-critical. We do not believe that we have a corner on the truth. It is because God is transcendent that human versions of theology are not. We practice *semper reformanda*, a continuing reformation, and we need multiple voices in order to do that well.

- We are called to practice community—a community of reverence, respect, dialogue, critical discourse, and care.

We invite all sorts of people to join us in our mission of education. Not all will accept once they hear what we are about. When hiring we need to ask, "Where are the people who are both concerned about justice and knowledgeable about economics?" "Where are the people who teach biology and practice living a less environmentally destructive lifestyle?" "Where are there people who teach religion and are willing to undertake the rebuilding of an orphanage in South Africa?" We may be interested even more in them when we discover that they are also Jewish, Muslim, Buddhist, or religiously hostile. I am ever so thankful for my colleagues who are Catholics and Quakers, Baptists and high Anglicans. But I am just as delighted by my colleague who is a religiously suspicious neo-Marxist, my colleague who is eclectically Buddhist and Christian, and my colleague who is sure there is no name for her spiritual practice. Ever more Lutheran colleges are now places where such persons are not merely welcomed, but valued.

CHAPTER FIVE

Rethinking the Lutheran University: Two Models

Introduction

It is my experience that a good deal of confusion arises in discussions about Lutheran higher education because of assumptions that are made. Many people interested in Lutheran higher education assume a particular model of what a Lutheran university should look like. Having made that assumption, they go on to judge the Lutheran character of particular institutions on how well they live up to that model. What I wish to do in this chapter is fourfold: First I want to make explicit what I believe is the most frequently assumed model. Second, I wish to show what the consequences have been (and are) of assuming this model, sketching both a brief history of the evolution of many Lutheran universities and colleges and a picture of the current situation. Third, I wish to show that there is at least one other model that should be considered and then develop that model more fully. Finally I wish to discuss the benefits and problems associated with these two models and make a proposal for the future.

The Seminary or "For Us/By Us" Model

A very common way to think about a Lutheran college or university is to think of it employing the paradigm of a seminary. A Lutheran seminary is quite naturally and appropriately education by Lutherans of Lutherans in Lutheranism for a Lutheran purpose. The purpose of such an educational institution is primarily the self-replication of Lutherans. By means of such institutions, pastors and teachers are trained for the future leadership of the church community. It is very natural and proper that this training should be done (at least primarily if not exclusively) by Lutherans and that it should be circumscribed by the confessions and practices of the Lutheran church.

History and Evolution of the Model

The seminary/pre-seminary model dominated the establishment and development of most of the Lutheran colleges and universities in the United States in the nineteenth century. A great many of them were founded as seminaries or as seminaries plus pre-seminaries. Many of them added teacher training to their curriculum early on; at some point they admitted women to the undergraduate college; and, as the institutions grew, they slowly came to add other practical and liberal subjects. But throughout this period of initial growth there was never any question about what the primary model was. They were institutions that practiced education of Lutherans, by Lutherans, focused on the preservation and support of a community of educated Lutherans.

At some point (and the date varies depending on geography and demography) many of these schools expanded their curriculum as their student populations grew. In many cases the seminary and pre-seminary students who were there became a minority, and the Lutheran students became a smaller percentage of the whole, sometimes even becoming a minority among the religiously identified students in the university. In many cases the same practices and patterns remained in spite of these other changes. The campus still had a focal worship space; the university still held daily or weekly chapel services; it still had a faculty in theology, perhaps slowly evolving into a faculty in religious studies. A substantial though diminishing number of faculty and administrators were Lutheran. The president and the board of trustees embodied and, nominally at least, sought to preserve some semblance of that original Lutheran identity.

As long as the for us/by us model continued to dominate thinking about Lutheran colleges and universities, there were predictable reactions to the historical shifts and changes noted above. Many alumni, church leaders, and leaders of these colleges and universities saw these changes and lamented them. It was easy to see that what had evolved was not "Lutheran" in the same way that the seminary/pre-seminary had been. It was clear, for example, that the institution was no longer primarily for Lutherans or by Lutherans, and it became quite clear that it was no longer predominantly for the preservation and promulgation of Lutheranism either. The judgments were commonly made, therefore, that these institutions had "lapsed," abandoned their Lutheran identity, or fallen into the "slough of secularism." Some presidents of some Lutheran colleges explicitly pronounced that, though their institutions had been "historically Lutheran," they were no longer Lutheran and had no interest in being so. They sought their identity elsewhere, often wishing to become an elite American private liberal arts college. Since the for us/by us model no longer fit, they denied the Lutheran connection altogether and sought a model from a different source. Some presidents and boards of trustees, on the other hand, sought to lead their institutions back in the direction of the earlier model. Some were confused rather thoroughly about whether they were or wanted to be a Lutheran university in that sense any more. They tolerated the memory of having been a Lutheran college for the sake of their older alumni, but did not press the idea in the presence of new students or current faculty, etc. They hoped "to be all things to all people" and avoided serious discussions of identity and mission whenever possible.

All of these judgments operate on the assumption that the for us/by us model is *the model* for Lutheran higher education. Some have sought to move back toward it, some have abandoned it, some are judged to have unintentionally "lapsed" from it, some have avoided discussion of it whenever possible, and some have been confused by it. But what, if it is not *the model*? What if there is another viable model of what a Lutheran college or university is or might be?

The Vocation Model

This is the "for the world with a lot of help from our friends" model. The university is a calling to serve (through the education of persons) the deep needs of the world. I call this the vocation model because it is based on Luther's understanding of vocation.

In the Christian world of the late Middle Ages the term vocation applied exclusively to people who had "a religious calling," i.e., it applied to people called away from the world to become monks, nuns, etc. Luther was one such person; he became an Augustinian monk and by all accounts pursued this religious life with utmost effort and great seriousness. But over the years Luther came to think of vocation in a very different way. He came to see that *all persons have a vocation*, a call from God to serve the real needs of their neighbors. This call applied as much to the peasant growing turnips as it did to the mother caring for children, to the shoemaker making shoes or the legislator making laws. The test for vocation was not "Are you doing something religious?" but "Are you serving in your station the real needs of your neighbor?" So rather than seeing the monk or nun as the paradigm of vocation, Luther came to see the ordinary work of ordinary people as the paradigm. He came to critique the monastic life precisely because it was exclusively devoted to religiousness, i.e., to improving one's standing in the eyes of God, while it did not serve the real needs of real people in society. Luther stated:

> Every person has a calling. While tending to it God is served. A king is doing God's work when he is at pains to look after the welfare of his people. So does a mother when she tends to the needs of her children . . . and a student when he applies himself to his studies. . . . When a maid milks the cows or the farmer hoes the field, they serve God more truly than all the monks and nuns. . . . If this could be impressed on common people every servant and every householder would dance for joy and praise God. . . . If everyone would regard their service to their neighbor as service to God the whole world would be filled with *Gottesdienst* [literally "god-service"; this is also the German word for the worship liturgy]. The king, the stable master, the kitchen servant, the child in school, these are really God's workers.

Luther's parishioners had a hard time adjusting to this shift in view that he introduced. They kept on thinking they ought to be doing something "really religious"—penance, pilgrimages, veneration of the saints, etc. But Luther kept telling them, "Do your work in love for those you are given to serve with the gifts at your disposal. Do all this focused on the needs of your neighbor, and God will in that activity be served and glorified."

A Homely Illustration

DeAne Lagerquist, a professor at St. Olaf College, has employed the following illustration: If God has called us to make shoes, we are not called to make shoes with little crosses on them or shoes embossed with Luther's seal. Instead we are called to make good shoes—shoes that serve well the needs of those that wear them. So while there is no need to make Christian shoes or Lutheran shoes, there is a need for serviceable shoes, well-fitting shoes, etc. We are doing the Lutheran thing not by doing something peculiarly religious or by making something marked with Luther's seal, but precisely by focusing our attention on the real needs that require service. As long as those needs are being well met, it is not important that the need be Lutheran, that those served be Lutheran, or that those who are employed in serving it be exclusively Lutheran. Lutheran hospitals, nursing homes, social service agencies, day-care centers, and schools may (and often do) embody such an understanding of vocation.

I find this illustration to be provocative and informative. But if we leave the illustration at this point, we may miss something important. Up to this point in the discussion, we may be left with the impression that the Christian Lutheran shoemaker is a generic maker of generic shoes just like any other shoemaker would make. But I think there is more to vocation than that. As shoemakers we are called to serve, in love, the real needs of the neighbor. But regarding this employment as a calling requires us to ask some hard and radical questions: Are people's wants the same as people's needs? Are wants a good index of needs in a society thoroughly manipulated by advertising and fashion? Are some kinds of shoes actually damaging to wearers? Are some demeaning? Do some shoes signal class and other differences that do not serve our needs for mutual respect and community? Thus, though there is no necessity in claiming a vocation to make Christian shoes, the idea of vocation will influence the kinds of shoes one is willing to make and market. So seeing one's life and work as vocation does make a difference (and frequently a profound one) to what one does as well as how and why one does it.

Institutional Vocation

Luther maintained that institutions and not just individuals had a divine calling insofar as they serve real human needs. The temptation, of course, is for institutions to become self-serving or for them to operate on behalf of the professionals that operate them rather than the public they were intended to serve. Thus we must continually voice questions about what end we are serving and how well we serve it. Does our justice system serve well the needs of those who need it, or is it designed to serve well the needs of attorneys? Does our health care system serve well the needs of those who need it most, or is it shaped by the agendas of HMOs, insurance companies, and health care professionals? Does our system of public education serve well the needs of those who come to it in direst need? Does our political system serve well the needs of the country and its citizens, or does it serve the needs of parties and partisans? None of these are easy questions. They reveal to us that our means frequently do not serve the ends they espouse, and our institutions often do not serve those they claim to serve.

The Vocation Model of a Lutheran University

So what would it mean for a university to be shaped by this understanding of vocation? First of all, it would imply that the university would pervasively and perennially keep in mind a cluster of vocational questions:

- What are the deep needs of the world that we are called to address through the process of education?
- What kinds of persons does the world need in order to serve these deep needs?
- What are the real needs of students who we are called to meet through this educational process?
- How do we educate such persons?
- What gifts (and limitations) do we bring to this task?

We need to ask these questions *pervasively* because it is tempting to make them the province of some special office or program in the university rather than informing the task of everyone. We need to ask these questions *perennially* because it is easy to fall into a pattern of doing something because that is how we have always done it. What this means is that a university built on this model will constantly be in the process of critically reviewing its mission, its priorities, its polity, its curriculum, and its pedagogy.

When I posed these questions to my students and a few colleagues I received a great flow of responses, like turning on a tap. It was exciting to hear, to say the least. I offer just a small sample of their answers to these questions:

What are (and will be) the deep needs of the world?

A pattern of life that is not wasteful, not consuming at such a rate that it cannot be globally generalized. A way of human life that is sustainable. A solution to global problems of poverty, starvation, lack of water, lack of sewage systems. A way to make economics serve to enhance human life, not make humans who serve economics. "Economics as if people mattered."

Same for politics. Avoiding the great isms that have been so massively destructive in the last few centuries. Discovering positive models of community and responsible leadership. National and international trust.

James Martin, in his book *The Meaning of the 21st Century*, identifies what he calls the "mega-problems of the twenty-first century." Among these he includes:

Global warming	Population growth
Catastrophic water shortages	Pandemic
Spreading deserts	Growth of shanty cities
Famine	Global migrations
Violent religious extremism	Global war
Runaway computer intelligence	A new Dark Ages

It's interesting to compare his list to the list my students and colleagues generated.

What kinds of persons does the world require in order to address and serve its deepest needs?

Peacemakers, critical and creative thinkers, people who think beyond chauvinisms and other over-simple either/or patterns, people who know how to live sustainably, preservers of multi-dimensional personhood, people devoted to justice, people practiced in long-term and large-view thinking, people who combine realism and hope, people who practice community.

How do we educate such persons?

Practice in critical thinking and civil critical discourse. Exercise in imagination, in thinking "outside the box." Practice in systems thinking, in analysis *and* synthesis, in team work and problem solving. Practice in global awareness, in being well-informed, in effective communication, in avoiding the tempting "easy answers" that so many in our culture seem to fall for.

What gifts do we (as a Lutheran university) bring to this task?

A gospel that liberates us for service to the world, an understanding of the creation as a gift, and an understanding of our own calling as stewards of the creation. Christ as a model of the human; the church as a model of honest yet hopeful community, diffracting God's love for the world. Models of critical faithfulness, loving reformation. A tradition of dialogical education at the intersection of faith, the disciplines, and the professions. A community of realism *and* hope.

Second, a university informed by this understanding of vocation would honor the work of all who perform essential tasks in the university as well as in society. We need to celebrate the callings of students as well as of teachers, coaches, and those who sweep the floors, of administrators and other maintenance personnel, and of secretaries and those who work in the library and bookstore. We should be wary of the ways we have of sorting jobs according to prestige, and we should be suspicious of all rigid categorizations (e.g., religious vs. secular, labor vs. management).

Third, we should evaluate ourselves on how well we serve those we are given to serve and be very suspicious of other ways of rating or ranking universities based on publications, funded research grants, percentages of applicants turned away, average ACT or SAT scores, etc. The question for the vocation-focused university is not "How elite are we?" but "How well do we do the task of educating those whom we are given to serve?" and "How well do our graduates go out to serve the needs of the world?"

Will this leave universities and colleges modeled on the vocational concept indistinguishable from generic secular institutions? I do not think so. If we may generalize on the past and present performance of our secular universities, I think we can say that they are not places that have been informed by the cluster of vocational questions cited above. Secular universities are very often dominated by the idea of disciplinary and sub-disciplinary specialization, professionalization, disciplinary reductionism, and economic utilitarianism. Seldom is the question raised about whether this pattern serves well the needs of society, the needs of students, or the deep needs of the world. Secular universities have fallen prey to and help perpetuate all sorts of elitism, chauvinism, and fashion-isms to which the vocation model would object and which it would attempt to avoid. As a consequence I believe that almost all the professional programs one can find in a university would be pursued differently if tested by the vocational questions cited above. I believe that many of the disciplines would be re-organized, many of the requirements would be re-thought, and a good deal of pedagogy would be re-considered as well.

But this does not imply that everything should be different. Lutherans do not have (nor should we want) an exclusive copyright on those vocational questions. It is possible that these vocational questions can be asked by others with keen insight and honesty, and that educational programs can be designed by others who have taken the service of real needs seriously. We should be happy when this is so and be willing to learn from them.

So which of these two models is better?

My own conclusion is that both are good. The for us/by us model was and may still be appropriate in situations where there is a fairly large community of Lutherans who make up the student body, faculty, and staff of the institution. In the U.S., Minnesota, the Dakotas, Iowa, Illinois, and Wisconsin may still have a sufficient density of Lutherans to make such a model work. Seminaries (in the ELCA at least) are now separate institutions. They may be located near or even contiguous to Lutheran colleges or universities, but by now they have completely separate institutional identities. Their presence and the presence of their students, their faculty, and their curricula no longer answer (nor address) the question of the university's Lutheran identity—at least not in the way they once did.

But many of our Lutheran universities now serve very diverse student populations while employing very diverse faculties to do so. The for us/by us model no longer works well there. But there is no reason why the vocation model could not. In fact, to a large degree, it is already working well in a number of Lutheran institutions across the country. It is for such institutions, serving diverse student groups with diverse faculty, that the vocation model works best. It has the capacity to meet a real need (the deep needs of the world and the real needs of its diverse students) with the gifts it has available. That is, for me, the defining character of vocation, this intersection of needs and gifts. Such a college or university has the capacity to be Lutheran in a significant sense, embodying as it does a key concept and understanding of Lutheran thinking.

The for us/by us model needs a large density of Lutherans, both in the student population and in the faculty and administration. Along with this density comes the almost unavoidable feeling that some of the faculty/administration are insiders and some outsiders. Non-Lutherans may be tolerated and even welcomed, but it is hard to escape the conclusion that they are welcome in spite of their not being "us" while clearly being one of "them."

Each of these models has strengths and certain limitations. The strongest arguments for the vocation model are:

1. Many of our colleges and universities that have considered themselves no longer Lutheran or marginally Lutheran because they no longer serve predominantly Lutheran students with predominantly Lutheran faculty now have occasion to re-examine that judgment and the assumptions on which it was based. Many of our colleges and universities may be more Lutheran than they thought they were.

2. It is a way of locating the Lutheran-ness of the institution in its primary task, the task of educating persons for service to the world, not in "the religious frosting" of the place.

3. It has implications for both curriculum and pedagogy. It is an understanding of education that can empower serious discussion about the why and the how of our efforts at educating.

4. It is a way of overcoming any distinction between insiders and outsiders. Educating students for service to the world is a task everyone can be enlisted to do, not just Christians, not just Lutherans, not just persons who see themselves as religious.

5. The vocation model provides us with a clear answer to the question, "Why should we invest ourselves in the survival and thriving of Lutheran colleges and universities?" It is not just out of loyalty and nostalgia. It is because these places offer a kind of education that the world desperately needs and that our students need.

The vocation model evaluates faculty and administration on their ability and willingness to be engaged in the work at hand. When I volunteered to work on a Habitat for Humanity project, no one asked me, "Are you a Christian, a Buddhist, or a Muslim?" They asked me, "Do you know how to frame a wall? Do you know how to install foam insulation? Have you ever plastered a seam of sheet-rock?" Given the vocation model of education, exactly the same thing is true. Once the work we are trying to do has been explained, the question becomes,

"Do you have the training, experience, and commitment to join us in this task? Right now we need someone who can teach bio-chemistry, logic, geriatric nursing, and Asian history. We need someone to run the boiler room, to manage the food service, to dean the law school, and to serve as university bursar."

A New Lutheran University?

It has been quite a while since anyone in the U.S. talked about founding a new Lutheran university. In the U.S. the last to be established was California Lutheran University, which came into being as a result of a large gift of land to the Lutheran church designated to be used for educational purposes. Why have there not been others? The main reason is, I believe, because of the prevalence of the assumption of the for us/by us model. Since, it was supposed, there are no longer dense populations of Lutherans not already served by one or more Lutheran schools, there is no perception of a need to establish more of them. But if we shift to the vocation model, we see that the answer to that question is not so obviously negative. Are there students who need to be well served in higher education? Yes, many of them. Are there still deep needs of the world that can be served by means of the education of these persons? Yes, clearly. Do Lutherans still have gifts to bring to this task? Yes, a host of them. Well then, should someone not be asking the question about the establishment of another Lutheran college or university? It would not need to be located in a place occupied by a bunch of Lutherans. It would only need to be a place where a need and an opportunity are present. Informed by the cluster of vocational questions we considered earlier, it would be an exciting place, a vital place, a creative place, and a world-serving place. I would not mind spending what years I have left as an educator in a place like that.

Afterthoughts

The problem with a "two models" approach to any question is the likelihood of supposing that those are the only two models or that they are exclusive. Neither of these needs be the case. It is very possible that someone may discern other models than the two presented here. In fact, I would be happy if that were the case. My own faint imagination does not see, at present, what they might be. But much more helpful, I believe, is the suggestion that these two models are, in fact two poles of a continuum and that most institutions find themselves some-where between the models sketched above. I can imagine many happy compromises between the two models. I think those compromises are more fruitfully made when we see clearly what the models are and are explicit about the ways in which our institutions are informed by each.

My occasion for writing this is the perception that for many institu-tions the for us/by us model has dominated our thinking without being explicitly aware of it and without being aware that there is another vi-able Lutheran model available. For too long the operative options have been either the for us/by us Lutheran university or the generic secular university. You're either A or B, in or out. I hope this discussion has shown that another very fruitful model is available.

CHAPTER SIX

The Freedom of the Christian College

Mark Tranvik of Augsburg College has commented about the dominant tendency in America to identify Christianity in terms of stereotypes. He writes:

> The result is that large segments of the American public associate religion with the alien imposition of authority. It is assumed that a "religious" school is dominated by a host of narrow-minded prohibitions which inevitably result in the curtailment of free and open discussion. Higher education in many mainline colleges and universities has tended to respond accordingly by soft-pedaling it's religious heritage. . . . Because we want the world to know that we are not Oral Roberts or Brigham Young or Liberty University, we unwittingly have allowed these institutions to define the parameters of the discussion.

Tranvik asserts that, on the contrary, the Christian faith liberates minds and lives. My thesis here is that Tranvik is right and that it ought to be one of the chief functions of Christian colleges, particularly Christian colleges in the Lutheran tradition, to illustrate that liberation.

Luther, in his famous treatise, "The Freedom of the Christian," wrote:

> A Christian is a perfectly free lord of all, subject to none. A Christian is a perfectly dutiful servant of all, subject to all. . . . Freed from the vain attempt to justify himself . . . [the Christian] should be guided by this thought alone . . . considering nothing but the need of the neighbor.

"The Christian [called to the task of education] is a perfectly free lord of all, subject to none." What would happen to our colleges and to us who work in them, if we truly believed that? How would this radical assertion of freedom transform what we do?

The Dimensions of Freedom Explored

In Disney's film, Pinocchio sings:

> I've got no strings to hold me down,
> To make me fret, to make me frown.
> I had strings, but now I'm free.
> There are no strings on me.

The irony of the story is, of course, that Pinochio is owned and kept in a cage by the cruel puppet master, Stromboli. Even when he is able to escape that confinement, he is easily led into a new form of servitude. We see our strings if they are connected to our limbs, but not if they are connected to our minds.

Diogenes of Athens, the Cynic, as he was called, claimed to be Athens' one free man. No job, no property, beholden to none, he walked the streets of the cities of Hellas shooting sacred cows. Legend has it that one day Alexander the Great found him sitting on a tub in the *agora*. Alexander said, "Are you Diogenes the philosopher?" He answered, "I am." "I am Alexander, king of Macedon." Diogenes said nothing. "Ask any thing of me and I will grant it," said the king. "Move your damn horse; he's blocking the sunlight," Diogenes replied.

Diogenes showed no respect for prestige, title, or power, and no concern for the things that occupied most people. When Plato pointed out to him that if he would be a bit more respectful of the rich, he would not have to wash lettuce for his lunch money, Diogenes replied, "If you washed lettuce for your living you wouldn't have to suck up to the rich."

When eating his lunch within the precinct of a temple he was arrested and asked to give an account of himself. He said, "I ate there because that's where I was hungry." When arrested for not bowing down before the statue of the god he said, "Didn't it ever occur to you that the god is also behind you?" He once said, "I pissed on the leg of the man who called me a dog. Why was he so surprised?"

John Dominic Crossan, in his provocative book, *Jesus: A Revolutionary Biography*, describes Jesus as "a Jewish peasant Cynic." When I first read that I was shocked by the description. Now I am not so sure.

What was Jesus doing? What kind of liberation was he announcing? What does the good news of the reign of God imply?

I have a colleague, recently retired, whom I had the privilege of watching in the classroom a few years ago. He had gotten his hands on 1950s editions of some old magazines—*Better Homes & Gardens, Saturday Evening Post, Look*. He brought them to class and showed his students the ads and articles. The articles had titles like "Helping Your Husband with His Career," "Entertaining for Success," "Housework and Happiness." The ads showing beautiful women in dresses and heels standing happily next to the new refrigerator, range, hot water heater, tile floor, and a sparkling Buick. After showing these to the students he said, "These were the lies that your grandparents were told." He then pulled out a stack of magazines from the 1980s. The articles were different: "Juggling Motherhood and Career," "Recognizing Midlife Passage Signs in Yourself and Your Husband," "Starting Your Own Retirement Account—Toward Security and Happiness," "Ten New Home Make-over Ideas from Europe's Hottest Designers," "Preserving the Natural Youthful Beauty of Your Skin." The ads had changed a bit, too, with more mini-vans, more get-away vacations, more ads for pharmacological help with stress, aging, etc. The teacher then said, "These were the lies that your parents were told."

Then he asked his class, "So, what are the lies that you're being told?" Students mentioned several things, mostly things other people believe. The teacher held up a cell phone or blackberry. "What's the lie that this is telling?" One of the students said, "They're not lies as long as we believe them." The old guy laughed cynically. Finally someone said, "We've got to believe something—otherwise why get up in the morning and go to work?" My colleague put the cell phone and the stack of magazines aside and said, "Now maybe we're ready to actually learn something."

After class I said, "You were pretty hard on them." He replied, "Jesus calls his disciples to cast out demons. What makes you think that is not a violent act?"

The Bible is full of admonitions against idolatry. We probably like to think that is no longer a problem for us. No one asks us to bow down before the image of Osiris, Ashtarte, Baal, Jupiter, or the divine emperor. But how about the divinities in this contemporary pantheon:

wealth; prestige; power; success; cool, hot, brand name stuff; drugged oblivion; national security? I have an acquaintance who has a whole room in his house set up as a shrine to the Pittsburgh Steelers. That is probably one of the less harmful of the gods one could worship these days.

Henry David Thoreau, an outspoken critic of slavery and the government that tolerated it, remarked about the "voluntary slavery" of many of his neighbors and contemporaries. "They say they are working to buy their farms," Thoreau commented, "but it seems to me their farms end up owning them. . . . The behavior of these so-called freemen only makes sense if you suppose that they are doing penance for some horrible sins committed in a former life. Though they suffer greatly from the work, they will not stop embracing the karma that binds them to it."

Doris Lessing's tiny book, *Prisons We Choose to Live Inside*, catalogues many examples of cases where communities and whole nations seem to choose to give their mindfulness and independence away in favor of securely "belonging in the group." She doesn't believe that humans will ever get over this tendency, but she thinks that education ought to make us recognize it and prepare us to stand against it.

That is the idea behind recognizing that certain patterns of thinking are fallacies. We understand that these patterns of thought are prevalent, tempting, and wrong. That is what a liberal (read "liberating") education ought to do. It ought to make us hear in our own words and see in our own actions patterns we should be beware of. My youngest son (then fourteen years old) sat with me as we watched President George W. Bush give his famous "evil empire" speech. Afterwards I asked him what he thought. His comment made me glow with pride, "He sounds like a man who has never read a Greek tragedy."

There is no lack of good teachers if we but hear them and connect them to our own lives and situations. How much can be learned from Sophocles and Euripides, Hosea and Amos, and the whole host of more recent witnesses to the un-freedom of the human animal? If we do not teach our students one more thing, we should teach them to see their own blindness and to name their own jailers and puppet-masters, to identify the idols in whose name they are being incarcerated.

The Idols of Academe

The university, of course, has its own idols and lies. One is told whenever we set up academic structures of disciplines and sub-disciplines which, having created their own jargon, end up not even being able to talk to one another. The impression we give ourselves and our students is that the world also is divided in these ways. The model for inquiry has become the factory assembly line where each worker fusses with one little part. The problem with this is that a kind of blindness for the whole sets in. We all beg off, saying, "That's not my specialty."

Back in the 1970s I began suffering from a bewildering array of health problems: severe arthritis, anemia, bone marrow problems, sudden weight loss, not enough energy to climb one flight of stairs, escalating cholesterol and triglyceride levels, and loss of vision. I was seeing a whole host of specialists. The arthritis doctor wanted to inject my joints with some gold compound; my blood doctor was talking about bone-marrow transplants; another doctor had placed me on a severe fat-restricted diet; the ophthalmologist kept doing retinal scans. The father of one of my students, a semi-retired missionary doctor, invited me to lunch one day and said, "Tom, you look really awful. Tell me what's happening with you." I told him the whole story, and he finally said, "Didn't it occur to any of your doctors that all of these things may be related? Hasn't anybody suggested that they may all be symptoms masking a single cause?" None of the specialists had looked in that direction. Their specialties had, in one sense, made them big-picture blind. Within a week he had ordered a CAT-scan of my head and discovered a tumor sitting on my pituitary gland right between my optic nerves. Within two weeks I had surgery, the tumor was removed, and I was on a path to healing. The arthritis symptoms went away, my blood problems abated, I started gaining weight and getting renewed energy, and my vision improved.

I am not making an argument against specialists. The surgeon was, after all, a specialist. What I am warning against is the fallacy that specialism exhausts reality. Early in the twentieth century Alfred North Whitehead argued that education occurs in a rhythm of three stages: the stage of youthful excitement that he calls romance, the stage of precision or discipline, and the stage of generalization or synthesis. He thought that we err as educators if we introduce the discipline stage too early, and we err most commonly in the modern world by skipping the last stage altogether.

Mark C. Taylor, in his *New York Times* op-ed piece, "End the University As We Know It," argues that the structure of departments, disciplines, and sub-disciplines should be replaced by a structure of webs focused on general problems such as language, media, money, life, and water. He writes:

> A Water program would bring together people in the humanities, arts, social and natural sciences with representatives from professional schools like medicine, law, business, engineering, social work, and architecture. Through the intersection of multiple perspectives and approaches, new theoretical insights will develop and unexpected practical solutions will emerge.

I tend to go with Whitehead here rather than Taylor. I do not think it is a matter of replacing the disciplines with the web-structure so much as it is making sure that narrowly trained specialists do not have the last word. Graduate education well might be revised to include at least a year at the end which a scholar devotes to working on some large, multi-dimensional problem with a team of other people. Perhaps this could be a year of national service that could help repay some of the costs of the scholar's education.

If such a program is not in place, then colleges and universities could build such work into the development programs for their own faculty. What might happen if faculty from education, psychology, sociology, religion, law, economics, political science, and nursing sat down for two months to understand and address "The school dropout rate of inner city youth," or "Urgent needs of aging citizens," or "Wasted energy"?

The Manifestation of That Freedom

In *The Gift and Task of Lutheran Higher Education* I wrote:

> Being critical is one of the manifestations of freedom. Christians are free to serve the world by being critical and by challenging all human claims to ultimacy. We are called, in other words, to recognize idols when we see them. This is not easy to do because most of us have been captured by some agenda our society has laid on us. . . . Certainly materialism in all its modes is one such idol. How often have we felt the temptation to believe that we are valuable

for what we have, for those things we call "our posses-
sions"? How frequently do all other concerns take a back
seat to economic progress? How tempting is the idea that
having more will bring us happiness and fulfillment? For
how many of us is success defined in terms of income and
consumption?

If we are Christians, we do not worship that god, nor do we have
any reason to follow its credo. A thoroughgoing skepticism and sus-
picion ought to accompany this and every other humanly constructed
claim to ultimacy. That critical stance is a service to our students and a
service to the world. How might we be doing that?

1. Lutheran colleges ought to be communities of vigorous critical discourse where the most serious issues and the most challenging
ideas are discussed. I commonly teach a senior course in ethics, and
I commonly ask my students where in public they have seen serious
ethical issues civilly discussed. In school? At home? At church? Over
ninety percent answer, "Nowhere." The college or university has the
opportunity to be the community's forum, to embody the dialogue
that Aristotle thought defined politics: "the public discussion of those
questions that matter most."

2. Students with music majors at my university are required to
attend a prescribed number of on-campus and off-campus musical
events per semester. I think the same kind of requirement ought to be
made of other students. We have the good fortune of being located in
the state capital. There are no lack of public hearings, committee meetings, trials, and council meetings that students could attend to see:

a. what issues are being discussed

b. what the arguments are that are considered

c. how well or badly the arguments are made

d. how decisions get made

Students who have witnessed the discussions on-campus can make
an interesting comparison.

3. Disciplines should be taught with time and attention for a critical view of what students have just learned. When I teach logic, it is
important that students acquire the tools of logical analysis and the

appropriate symbol systems that embody it. But it is also important that they become aware of what the limits of such analysis are and the temptations thinkers have fallen into when they thought that the predicate calculus was *the* language of responsible discourse. When I teach ethical theory, it is important to see what the use of such theoretic tools accomplishes. But I must not allow students to leave thinking that knowing such theories is the sum total of ethical thinking. In the law school it is important that students learn the law and how to negotiate the institutions that embody it. But somewhere before the end of the process students should be encouraged to talk about those whom those institutions serve badly and the ways in which legal processes may not serve the ends of justice and order at all.

Freedom from and Freedom to

Freedom from the lies, demons, and idols that so frequently control our lives is only the first part of Luther's discussion of freedom. Having gained that liberation, we are now free to see the need of our neighbor and serve it. Buddhists talk about the three dimensions of awakening:

1. liberation from *samsara* (illusion)

2. extreme joy and release

3. deep compassion

Some critics of both Luther and Buddhism complain: "You offer freedom with one hand but take it away with the other. What kind of freedom does 'the servant of all' really have?" I think that is a legitimate criticism provided that one makes an assumption, namely that it is possible for a person to serve no master. If that is possible, then getting rid of every master, every obligation, and every value would be ultimate freedom. That is, I believe, what Diogenes had in mind. He seems to serve no other master except for his own freedom. He is a citizen of no *polis* but the cosmos, which leaves him free of all responsibility. Is "freedom from," by itself, a worthy goal of a whole life?

Both Buddhists and Christians would reply that therein lies a very large temptation—the temptation to believe that the self (who will be in charge when all the other masters have been chased out) is not itself an idol and an illusion. The Buddhists certainly think so, and Christians do so as well. St. Paul writes about the necessity of putting the old self to death in order that the Christ-self might live in us: "We are baptized into Christ's death . . . to be raised again with him." "It is not I who live," Paul writes, "but Christ who lives in me." And, "Therefore if anyone is in Christ he is a new creation. The old has passed away and the new has come." (Romans 6:3, 8; 2 Corinthians 5:17). An image I like is to think of the self as a glass that most of the time reflects the values and priorities of the culture. But turned in a different way, the glass can become a prism. The powerful light of God's love enters on one side, and the full spectrum is refracted out into the world on the other. God's love transforms us into agents of loving service in the world. Illumination becomes vocation.

These two themes—freedom from and freedom to, or freedom and vocation—should characterize education in a Lutheran college and university. It would be the most critical and liberated of communities, on the one hand, and the most caring and serving, on the other.

CHAPTER SEVEN

Who Needs a Lutheran College/University? The Question Explored and Answered

I have responded to this question differently at different times. When most of our Lutheran colleges and universities were founded, the answer would have been, "We need Lutheran colleges and universities to train Lutheran pastors and teachers to serve the communities of German, Scandinavian, or Finnish immigrants coming into the country." A little later the answer probably would have been, "We need Lutheran colleges and universities to help the children and grandchildren of those immigrants blend into the American mainstream at the same time that we remind them of their ethnic and religious heritage." That answer served for quite a long time. But both of those answers assume that a Lutheran university is basically a for us/by us operation, that it is an institution for Lutherans by Lutherans serving Lutheran purposes. I think that is a model that still does apply to Lutheran seminaries. It may still apply at a college or two. In many Lutheran colleges today, however, where Lutherans are a minority of the student body and the faculty and the staff, the for us/by us model doesn't serve well any more.

So, we will ask the question again, slightly expanded: "Who needs a Lutheran college/university, and why?" Here are some other possible responses:

1. We do not really need them. There are plenty of good schools of different kinds. Some of them such as community colleges and on-line universities, are growing at a tremendous rate.

2. We need them because we have them. Every institution has in it some tendency to self-preservation even without knowing why. So, it may be thought, we have as much right to exist as anyone in the marketplace.

This answer is often accompanied by the belief that a Lutheran college ought to become just another generic institution, offering generic courses toward generic majors leading to generic degrees. This view must be tempting because I hear it from so many quarters, but I am convinced that becoming generic educational unit generators would be the worst mistake we could make. If students and their parents begin to perceive Lutheran colleges in this way, then they will eventually ask themselves: "Where can I get these generic credits at the lowest possible price?" If we try to play the generic game, we will lose at it. It will end up with us trying to compete with the educational Walmarts of this world. Students will leave, transfer out, or transfer in randomly because the college has no identity and no value to offer. The graduates produced will have no more loyalty than I do to the market where I shop for the best price on toilet paper.

3. There are not really any Lutheran universities any more, there are just "historically Lutheran universities." They used to be Lutheran in the sense of being for Lutherans and by Lutherans, but they pretty much have evolved out of existence.

I do not think this is true, but it is a view I have heard colleagues give, so I suppose it is worth voicing here.

4. We need them because some of us have a nostalgia for them. There are still loyal alumni and supporters that remember the Lutheran connection. Thus it gets trotted out at homecoming and other times when alumni are likely to be present, but not often otherwise.

If we polled members of boards of trustees or alumni boards at our colleges, my guess would be that most of them would give some answer like that.

5. We need them because we (faculty and staff) work at them and we need jobs.

6. We need them because they are somewhat like places we admire and emulate (elite liberal arts colleges; small, caring, family-oriented colleges with ivy; etc.). They are places where we are happy to work while we are waiting for that call from Harvard or Cal Tech or whatever institution is on your dream list.

None of these responses are very good reasons for the existence of Lutheran colleges. Some of them are false; others are based on bad assumptions. None of these reasons are good enough to inspire a reflective person to devote her/his life, best energies, or life savings to them. None of them are good enough to make anybody want to start a new Lutheran university or to invest in making one thrive and grow.

But to say that these are not good or essential or inspiring reasons is not equivalent to saying that there are no good reasons. The reality is that these reasons, though frequently at the top of the sack of popular thought about the reason for the existence of Lutheran colleges are not good reasons.

So, for the third time, we ask the opening question: Who needs a Lutheran college/university? Here is how I would answer:

1. We need colleges/universities that embody what Luther called "the freedom of the Christian." Freed from having to earn the love of God, we are free to be fully and honestly human. Freed from the need to be someone else, we are free to be ourselves. We have no need to deny the body in service of some spiritual purity; we have no need to depart the natural to serve the supernatural. We can be, as Luther certainly was, bodily and earthly and thoroughly creaturely. We are also freed from the rule of the world's self-constructed hierarchies. We are freed to be women, not "not quite men;" to be students, not "not quite careered;" to be secretaries and custodians and steam engineers, not "not quite executives;" and even to be philosophers, not "not quite theologians."

Freedom is, I believe, the first premise of genuine education. Without that premise schooling just becomes a sucking up to some cultural agenda, being a success, being cool, or being in. To witness the absence of such freedom one only has to visit any high school in America or perhaps any elite university and see the anxieties that prevail there. Without freedom—the radical freedom Luther was talking about—schooling is not education at all but a training to be a drone in the great social hive.

2. We need universities that embody Luther's own penchant for what I have called *critical faithfulness*. A Lutheran university should be a critical and self-critical place; a place that challenges the cultural, political, economic and religious assumptions and institutions of the age. Luther did that (and got in deep trouble for it), yet he was not critical in the way a cynic is critical (seeing through everything and commit-

ted to nothing). He was critical while being thoroughly engaged and thoroughly caring about the things he critiqued. He was a loving critic and a faithful critic, and I think we should follow his model. As an implication of this we need to be universities that regularly stop and ask, "What are the idols of this age? What are the things that most people seem to assume? What are those assumptions built into our ways of seeing and knowing the world, that are built into our disciplines? What are the assumptions built into our culture's models of success and into our understanding of what it means to be human?" The boldness and openness to pose questions of this sort ought to be characteristic of a Lutheran university.

3. We need universities that have deep historical and theological reasons for taking the education of the whole person seriously. There are so many forces in our contemporary world that want to reduce us to objects, ciphers, or our roles as producer and consumer. We badly need places that critique such reductionisms and that show what whole human regard is all about. There are many institutions that use the rhetoric of "holistic education," but very few that actually take that seriously. Even our disciplines and professions may be reductionistic. We need universities that educate toward an enlarged and multi-dimensional humanity not toward a narrowed and flattened humanity. We need universities that connect scholarship to teaching and connect both to the personal growth of the student. Research universities cannot even connect the first two and can make no sense of connecting the latter.

4. We need universities that have deep, theological reasons for taking earth stewardship seriously. When I was a student this was not even on anyone's awareness screen. I honestly think I was in my late twenties before I ever heard anyone talk about sustainable agriculture or an ecological footprint, to say nothing of ideas like global warming or eco-justice. We were for a very long time ecologically blind, and then for a long time we have been in a state of ecological denial. As people informed by the Genesis story of creation, we should have been awake to this all along. The call to be the steward (not the possessor) of creation is there in the first two chapters of Genesis. Yet people who supposedly take that text seriously have been and continue to be complicit in the destruction of the creation. We need to ask why the most vocal so-called "creationists" are not also the leading voices for earth stewardship. The wasting and the destruction of God's world,

the world God declares over and over again to be good, is not only bad science and stupidly short-sighted economics, it is blasphemy — wantonly abusing and wasting God's lavish gift of creation. One of my favorite authors, Wendell Berry, has expressed it thus:

> Too often modern Christianity is still at bottom the religion of Miss Watson, intent on a dull and superstitious rigmarole by which we can avoid going to "the bad place" and instead go to "the good place." One can hardly help sympathizing with Huck Finn when he says, "I made up my mind I wouldn't try for it." . . . Modern Christianity has become willy-nilly the religion of the state and the economic status quo. Because it has been so exclusively dedicated to incanting anemic souls into heaven, it has allowed itself to become the tool of much earthly villainy.

We need people and institutions that take earth stewardship seriously, learning to celebrate the gifts of creation and learning to be caretakers of it.

Of course we must be learners in this regard at the same time that we are teachers. It certainly is not the case that my generation can teach this younger generation how to live sustainably. We must make confession (of both ignorance and responsibility) and then become a community of learners. This is my favorite definition of a teacher anyway: "A teacher is a communicative learner."

5. We need universities that have agendas for taking peace, justice, compassion, and forgiveness seriously. We can do that in courses and programs such as peace studies, studies about political and economic justice, etc., but we can also do this in the very basic ways in which we treat each other. We can make each other feel welcome; we can reach out to those who have been hurt in one way or another; we can provide support for those who are struggling; we can give opportunities to begin again. The early church was noted by both its supporters and its critics as a radically inclusive community, a place where all kinds of distinctions of utmost importance in the empire counted for nothing: Were you rich or poor, slave or free, citizen or alien, male or female, Jew or Greek? This combination of things (reaching out to the outsider, dwelling in peace, seeking justice, practicing compassion, forgiveness) creates a bundle that Nick Wolterstorff has called by the Hebrew word, *shalom*. It is his and my belief that universities like this ought to be a bit

different because they are embodiments of a different view of what it means to be human, to be humans in the world and to be humans with humans. To be in a world without humans, to be in a world where no one treats you as a human—that is a horror story of the worst imaginable sort. Yet it is not just imagination because it is a story that has been played out in the gulags, concentration camps, killing fields, and sweat shops that we have witnessed again and again in the last century.

6. We need universities that have a calling to serve by means of education the deep needs of the world. One of Luther's key ideas was his understanding of vocation. He believed that every human is called to do God's work. Unlike most of his contemporaries, he did not understand God's work to be the doing of something peculiarly religious. One does God's work by doing in love something that serves the real needs of persons at hand.

How does Luther's understanding of vocation apply to the university? Luther's understanding of vocation makes us see learning as ultimately focused on service. Our culture is most likely to see learning as a training to be a commodity: "We need workers for the world economy," our leaders say. If we see the world as a world of jobs, our view is limited in a certain way. All you have to do is read the want ads for a few weeks to get a feeling for what that world looks like. We have a vocation wherever the gifts we possess intersect with the needs of the world. To view the world as an intersecting world of needs and gifts expands our vision and expands our view of the possibilities. Someone saying, "It's not my job," expresses a very different relationship to the world than someone saying, "It needs to be done."

Another common view of the justification of learning is seeing it as a ticket to elite society and high culture. With education I can enjoy the best concerts and converse about the best books with the best people in the nicest places. It is a tempting view, but not one that Luther would buy.

A third and less common view sees learning as an end in itself, something done just for the joy of it. Luther recognizes the appeal of this, having felt such joy himself, but he also sees it as something of a temptation embodied in the monastic ideal that the highest human calling is a life of pure contemplation. So he reminds us that learning also ought to serve the needs of the world, the real needs of the neighbor.

In contrast to all these views, Luther's concept of vocation makes us look at all education as potentially focused on service. Luther's concept of vocation should make us critical of the professions, our institutions, and the ways we have of preparing people for them. Examples:

Law school trains attorneys and other legal professionals.

Education departments train education majors for certification in education.

Pre-med and nursing programs train people for health professions.

But in each case we need to stop and ask: How do these professions and institutions serve the deep needs of the world? Do they serve well the needs of those who come to them in deepest need? Are these professions and the institutions that embody them really serving the needs of the professionals who work in them and not primarily those who come to them in need? Are we educating reflective professionals who serve, or are we training self-serving professionals?

The idea of vocation as an idea shaping education should lead us to see education in a different way—a way more expansive, more focused, and more critical both of the needs of students and the needs of the world. *The Washington Monthly* ranked colleges and universities, citing both openness to economically disadvantaged students and the service records of graduates among the ranking criteria. Needless to say the rankings turn out quite different than the *U.S. News & World Report* ranking does (where one can increase one's ranking by refusing to admit a larger percentage of one's applicants). Interestingly eight of the twenty-eight ELCA colleges are listed in *Washington Monthly's* top 100. By the *U.S. News* rankings only two are in "the elite 100."

Many of the things I have described as characterizing Lutheran universities are in our root stock because they are biblical (like the ideas of *shalom*, earth stewardship, and whole personhood). Some are there because they are Christian (like the understanding of radical inclusiveness and compassion). Still others are there because they are peculiarly Lutheran (like critical faithfulness and the idea of vocation as service of the deep needs of the world). It is not important that any of them are exclusively ours. It is important that we take them seriously (not to say that no one else does).

Coda: So, Who Needs a Lutheran College/University?

I think that the answer (or at least a good part of it) is now becoming plain. If we are what we claim to be as Christian colleges and universities in the Lutheran tradition:

1. *The world* needs such places, for they are places that perennially articulate those deep needs and find ways, through education, to produce humans that can address them.

2. *Our students* need them—not only students who are open to seeing life as a calling to service, but also students who thought they were here just to get a degree, then find themselves called to something more. ("I came here to get a degree, but I ended up getting an education.") For such students the university years are years of growth as persons, years of transformation of vision, years of calling—all of these honed against the stone of a particular discipline.

3. *The professions and our disciplines* need them because both need places where they can be pursued critically and self-critically, honestly and humanly.

4. *The church* needs them for it is in such places that we begin to realize what it means in the contemporary world to "love our neighbor as ourselves." Like the very religious young man in the Good Samaritan narrative in the Gospel of Luke who comes to Jesus asking about the path to eternal life, the church (and in fact religious people everywhere) is tempted to focus on the love of God and miss the needs of the neighbor, miss the gifts we have to share in serving such needs, and miss the dimensions of neighborliness altogether. The Good Samaritan story that Jesus tells is played out for us over and over again in the lives of our students and the people they go on to serve. The love of God is not realized through an exclusive occupation with God, but through a refracting of God's love into the world.. Christians and other religious folk need to see this. Our Lutheran colleges and universities are places where they could see this if they looked.

5. *You and I* need them. I should not speak for you, I suppose, but I am excited by the prospect of a university distinguished by these themes: Christian freedom, critical faithfulness, education toward whole personhood, earth stewardship, and vocation. A place that took

such ideas seriously would be a great place to learn, an exciting place to teach, and a challenging place to serve.

In conclusion let me say that I think that these are good reasons for the Lutheran colleges universities we have. They are also good reasons for universities to take their Lutheran-ness seriously and for all of us to rejoice when they do.

We need education. Human societies cannot become human without education, and we certainly cannot reach our full potential as humans without it. But education, considered all by itself, is not sufficient. Germany, in the decades preceding and following World War I, was one of the most highly educated countries in the history of the world, but their sophisticated education was not sufficient to prevent one of the worst tragedies in human history. In fact the kind of highly scientific and technical education they had mastered coupled with the world-view that dominated that culture produced the conditions for monstrosity. It is not just education that is needed but an education of a particular sort. I would argue that the critical, free, and vocational focus that Lutheran higher education can have is exactly what the world and our students need. We should not be in the generic education business. We should be a Christian college/university shaped by the Lutheran tradition.

CHAPTER EIGHT

Educating the Whole Person

What Happens When a Philosopher Reads the Mail

When my youngest daughter neared her high school graduation, she was the recipient of stacks of mail from colleges and universities all across the country, public and private, well-known and previously unheard of. It has been fun for me to look through these letters, books, and even the DVDs sent by some. It is fascinating to see how colleges and universities make their pitch to prospective students in words and pictures. These mailings show a good deal about how these institutions view their student pool. The materials also tell the viewer a bit about the college/university that sent it, though not as much as one might suppose. If the name of the institution were blanked out on these fliers, how many of them could be identified by the pictures and descriptions that are included? One can make some pretty good guesses based on geographical hints—the one with the palm trees and stretches of white beach is more likely to be Eckerd College than it is to be St. Olaf—but the rest of the stuff is amazingly generic. Maybe generic sells?

One of the frequent parts of this generic pitch has been for colleges (less so for large public universities) to make the claim that they educate the whole person. "We educate body, mind, and spirit," some say, "enabling growth in heart and mind." "Where the intellectual you, the social you, and the private you become one," one institution put it. Some refer to this education as holistic; some refer to the education of the whole person. The language is not always the same, and the accompanying photos often make one wonder how the language connects to the reality, but the frequency of similar references made me a bit curious.

Why is this such a common part of the self-description of American colleges? Do we assume that college is a place where one will become a whole person? Does anyone take this language seriously? Does it shape curriculum? Does it shape pedagogy? Does it influence which faculty the institution tries to hire or the ones it promotes? Is anyone on these campuses responsible for articulating what "the whole person" means?

One evening, I spent a couple hours exploring the websites of many of the colleges represented in my daughter's stack. What I wanted to find was *any* indication that these questions were answered or even pursued. It would have been so nice to find that if I clicked on the words "holistic" or "whole personhood" or "growth in heart and mind," I would have found a page where all this was explained or engaged. What I found instead was a kind of silent assumption, namely that everyone knew what this meant and, therefore, no one needed to explain it. I pointed this out to my daughter, and she responded, "Oh, Dad, you take things so seriously. That's the trouble with being a philosopher: you suppose that people even *want* to mean what they say."

Maybe she is right. It would not be the first time. Ever since Socrates walked the streets of Athens, philosophers have been asking people to explain what they mean on the assumption that they really meant it. Socrates asked, since citizens had charged him with impiety, that someone should give a coherent account of what piety and impiety were. They did not, yet they convicted and executed him. So, I guess I stand in that tradition. Yet I put a good deal less at risk than Socrates did. All I am asking of these educational institutions is that someone should give an account of what whole-personhood is and what education for it should really look like. Is that too much to ask?

Maybe so. The university where I teach has completed a long process of writing a strategic plan. Guess what? The language of educating the whole person shows up there. I fired off a couple of e-mails saying, "Let's not talk this way unless we're willing to explain what this really means." But it is almost as though the language is chosen because it sounds good yet says nothing. That sounds like the definition for euphemism, doesn't it?

Sometimes "whole person" talk is a way of justifying required courses in physical education, health, religion, or something else. Those are not bad things to include in the curriculum. Better yet might be to include studies and practices that unite body, mind, and spirit, like dancing, yoga, playing a sport, or participating in the Japanese tea ceremony or the Christenson wine ceremony. But there is so much more that such rhetoric could mean and could imply. Or—my great fear—it can mean nothing. I write this in the hope that, for my own university community at least, it should mean something substantial.

Wholeness and Its Lack

In order to notice the lack of wholeness, one must have a notion of what the whole is. I can say to someone, "But you don't know the whole story" only if I know the story is larger than they know. I recognize a semi-circle because I have a pretty good image of what the circle, of which this is the part, looks like.

But it is equally true that we cannot describe wholeness if we do not know some common ways in which something can fail to be whole. A pie is not whole if it has slices missing, but it is also not whole if it is missing a filling or a crust or if it is "half baked." Some things lack wholeness in one or two ways. But some things, humans especially, can lack wholeness in many dimensions. There are some trivial senses in which a person could be less than whole—e.g. being an amputee or lacking a fairly essential human capacity such as the ability to speak. There are even some capacities which, if missing, make us doubt whether the being is human at all. Consequently we talk about an unfortunate individual "in a sustained vegetative state."

What are the kinds of lack of wholeness? Let's try an inventory:

1. *Fractionality* — A thing can be less than whole by missing some of its essential parts.

2. A thing can be less than whole by lacking an essential dimension; this we might call being *narrowed* or *flattened*, or being *shallow* or *superficial*.

3. A thing can be less than whole by being *undeveloped, retarded,* or *arrested*.

4. A thing can be less than whole by being *broken, fractured, fragmented,* or *disintegrated*.

5. A thing can be less than whole by being *handicapped* or *disabled*.

6. A thing may be less than whole by becoming *disconnected, separated,* or *alienated* from what sustains it.

7. A thing may be less than whole by *losing its life*, becoming *devitalized* or *de-activated*.

8. A person can be less than whole by failing at the task of achieving her/his calling. This is what Aristotle calls *a-psychia*. Erazim Kohak, a contemporary philosopher, writes, "Being human is not just a matter of being a member of a species . . . it is a task to which we are called. . . . Humans can be in-human, dogs cannot be in-dog."

There may be more than these eight ways of losing wholeness. Some of the above apply to objects, some only to living and growing things, and some to things that are active. But all of these senses, I would submit, apply to being human. Humans can fail to be whole in at least these many ways. Whether the list is complete or not, it shows us what a complex and multi-dimensional thing human wholeness is.

Academe Undermines Wholeness — Some Testimonials

All education does not lead to wholeness. In fact, some education leads in the opposite direction. Sharon Dalos Parks writes, ". . . professors [and many other highly educated professionals] have been and are particularly vulnerable to functioning as less than whole persons."

My colleague, Dr. Andrea Karkowski, responding to my question about why more faculty had not turned out to hear the poet laureate of the United States on our campus said, "You should remember, Tom, that many of us are trained in disciplines that require a diminished humanity."

Parker Palmer writes:

> My depression was partly the result of my own schooling, partly due to the way I was formed — and deformed — in educational systems of this country, to live out of the top inch and a half of the human self.

> We are a culture that values mastery and control. But in the shadow of these values lies a profound sense of isolation from our human wholeness. . . . It is only human to trade our wholeness for societal approval. . . . Education at its best . . . is not just about getting information or getting a job. Education is about healing and wholeness. It is about empowerment, liberation, transcendence, about increasing and renewing the vitality of life.

And Steven Glazer writes, "Education can serve as the core of a lifelong journey toward wholeness, but more often it is merely a random accumulation of facts, figures, and skills."

Some years ago, a colleague of mine serving with me on a committee excused himself from the conversation which had come round to the discussion of a difficult ethical issue. He said, "I have nothing to say here because ethics is not my specialty." I responded, "We don't talk about ethics because its our specialty, we talk about ethics because we are human."

Many of us feel uncomfortable when we are called upon to socialize with students, for example, as part of the welcome to new students during their orientation days. We feel vulnerable when we encounter them person to person, unprotected by the shelter of the podium, our notebook full of lecture notes, and our expertise. Naked and un-armed, we are required to meet another person.

Academe Undermines Wholeness—A Catalogue

1. We break reality into disciplinary categories and sub-categories and frequently offer them to the learner as if they had nothing to do with each other. Mark C. Taylor, in a provocative *New York Times* essay, "End the University As We Know It," suggests that disciplinary studies be supplanted (or at least supplemented) with what he calls "problem focused clusters." He suggests, for example, an academic focus called "Water," which would bring geologists, biologists, physicists, economists, political scientists, philosophers, historians, and students of religion to the table.

2. Academe leads students to believe, like most of their professors, that becoming a specialist expert is the end of education. The academic ideal at many institutions is to learn more and more about less and less. The titles of dissertations attest to this. Is the increased bacterial count in underwear worn for several days or the use of footnotes in the works of medieval philosopher Duns Scotus really the culmination of an education? I remember the despair of a former student of mine who lamented the grind of her dissertation work. She said, "I'm writing about such a tiny topic in which I have little real interest. It was the big questions, the existential questions, that first attracted me to the study of religion. But it's like no one is allowed to ask them anymore at this level. We're all pressed to become sub-specialists."

3. Bloom's taxonomy of cognitive development catalogues six different levels of thinking and learning. But there are several studies that show that about eighty-five percent of academic learning even at the

college level focuses only on the first level, the learning and repeating of information. If that is true, it serves to reinforce a flattened curriculum. The curriculum may contain a whole lot of information about a whole lot of things, but if all of the learning is informational, the education produced may be a mile wide but an inch deep. A whole education would include understanding, application, analysis, engagement, criticism, and creative synthesis. A flattened curriculum also produces a flattened thinker to deal with it. A person may be extremely well-informed, particularly in this electronic age, but if the person does not know how to understand, analyze, evaluate, apply, and synthesize this information, it cannot really become knowledge.

4. By focusing learning in courses, in classrooms, in departments, and in schools, we reinforce the idea that these things have little connection to "the real world" or to the student's development.

Education has become the consumption of academic units connected in no essential way to those who consume them. Yet we claim, in our literature, to be "transforming lives through education." For how many of our students does this occur? How many connect their learning to their lives, to the problems of the world or to the communities in which they live and work? Learning, because it is institutionalized in the way it is, also frequently gets separated from the world it ought to serve.

Models of the Human

The outcome of every process of education is some kind of human being. But what kind of human? Is it, as president George H.W. Bush said, "persons to compete effectively in global markets"? Is that the human we want? Or is such education, as Thomas Merton put it, "the mass production of people literally unfit for anything except to take part in an elaborate charade?"

The Technocrat

David Orr, in his provocative book, *Earth in Mind: On Education, the Environment and the Human Prospect,* contrasts the educational system that produced Albert Speer, chief architect and armaments engineer of the Third Reich, with the education system that produced Aldo Leopold, American conservation biologist and one of the earliest voices of the environmental movement.

Speer's education was the very best scientific education the world had to offer. He graduated with degrees from universities in Karlsruhe, Munich, and Berlin. The result of this education, Orr points out, was a generation without defenses for the seductions of Hitler and the new technologies of the Nazi regime. Toward the end of his life Speer wrote these plaintive words: "The tears that I shed are for myself as well as for my victims, for the man I could have been but was not, for a conscience I so easily destroyed."

Leopold's education, by contrast, produced a man capable of challenging the basic assumptions of both his culture and the education he had received. He had been trained as a wildlife manager but soon came to see the animals he tended as spiritual companions, the natural areas he surveyed as his teacher, and himself as a steward of an incredible gift. Both Speer and Leopold received a scientific education, but there was something about Speer's education that made the death of conscience and the death of a questioning awareness possible. At the same time there was something about Leopold's education (whether at university or from his family or from his long walks in nature) that kept his questioning and wondering self alive.

The Consumer

Every educational effort has, somewhere embedded deep within it, an anthropology, i.e. an image of the human toward which education moves. Any culture may have more than one such image, but it is important to recognize what the dominant image is. So, what is the image of the human that pervades American culture and education? If it were to be articulated, here is what I think it would say:

We, humans, are real in proportion to what we have. Those who have nothing truly run the risk of being nobody. We are free in proportion to our ability to obtain our wants. Our identity is basically that of a consumer. We work in order to earn money. We earn money in order to buy stuff. We have stuff in order to manifest our freedom and our identity. We need things that will tell us and others who we are. As the things we have grow old or out of fashion they become invisible. ("I don't have a thing to wear.") New clothes and gear are like social life preservers. Without them we will sink into a sea of nothingness. Besides the need for identity-giving things, we also have a need for entertainment, something to occupy our minds lest we have to notice reality. Education should provide us with the means to get good jobs, i.e. jobs that will allow us to live lives of well-entertained consumers. The having of these things is what it means to be a success.

This consumerist model of the human has at least three problems associated with it.

1. It gives us a shallow and one-dimensional picture of what it means to be human. A person who literally is what he/she has is a mannequin. A mannequin is built to display clothes and other accessories. It truly is what it has. But the last time I checked there are no mannequins worth getting to know. Apart from the stuff he/she displays, there is no one there—no mind, no soul, no personality, no one who can plan a life, have a genuine concern, show care, or take an idea seriously. They may be hot, cool, and/or sophisticated, but are they human? No.

2. The consumerist model of the human makes all human relationships competitive, or it makes us begin to use each other as accessories in the social identity Olympics. Cool, handsome, or beautiful friends are a kind of human jewelry. Shown off in the right place they help us get noticed. They help us attain and maintain reality.

3. The consumerist lifestyle consumes the earth and its resources. Contemporary Americans are the most environmentally destructive and wasteful humans who have ever lived. Is that the human we have aligned our educational institutions to produce? We often divide the globe between the developed, the developing, and the undeveloped. The assumption is that everyone wants to and should move toward the lifestyle that we, the developed world, model. India and China, the two most populous nations on earth, are quickly advancing into the developed category. That should make us all feel good, right? The answer that resource scientists all over the world are giving us is a clear, "No." The planet cannot survive huge numbers of people living high consumption lifestyles. So let's convince all of *them* to stop. The planet can afford only a few high consumption lifestyles and they, clearly, should belong to us. Right? I do not think so.

The Seeker of Oblivion

So, Albert Speer, the soulless technocrat, is not the model of the human we want. Neither is the successful consumerist, nor even the "wannabe" consumerist many of us, if we are honest, yearn to be. There are a few other models that seem to be common, particularly among the young. The person who uses drugs, alcohol, or extreme forms of entertainment as a way to find diversion and oblivion is surely one of them. There are lots of kids in college who seem to be pursuing that path. I can understand it only as a kind of anaesthesia, an attempt to dull the pain or anxiety of life.

The Dutiful Drudge

Another common pattern is the life of the person who works and works without stopping to wonder why. A frequent example of this is the parent who basically "lives for their kids" so that those children can become parents who indulge their kids, *ad infinitum*. This seems to work until someone asks, "Is this all there is?" I attended a funeral of a man about whom the only thing anyone said as a eulogy was, "He was a good provider."

Remember the lyrics to the song, "Whistle While You Work," sung by the dwarfs in Disney's movie *Snow White*?

> We dig dig dig dig dig dig dig from early morn to night.
> We dig dig dig dig dig dig dig up everything in sight.
> We dig up diamonds by the score,
> A thousand rubies, sometimes more.
> We don't know what we dig them for.
> We dig dig digga dig dig. . . .

Hard work and sacrifice for the kids—it almost sounds like an admirable ethic. We do not like to hear it questioned. But of course its just consumerism with a less offensive face. If these are not the models of the human that inspires students' and teachers' efforts at education, then what should be? Do we have something better to offer?

David Orr, in *Earth in Mind*, has written:

> The plain fact is that the world does not need more successful people. But it does desperately need more peacemakers, healers, restorers, story tellers, and lovers of every kind. It needs people who live well in their places. It needs people of moral courage . . . . And these qualities have little to do with success as our culture defines it.

Biblical Images of the Human

The opening chapters of Genesis tell a story about how we, humans, are related to the created world and to the creator. If we read this story with some care we can discover many things about ourselves:

1. We discover that we are creatures, a part of (not apart from) the creation, a creation that God declares to be good. The creation does not belong to us. It is not ours to do with as we please. It is our home, our source, but not our possession. Even what we are called, "humans" (*adamah* in Hebrew), means "from the earth."

2. We discover that we are called into conversation with the Creator. The whole of the Bible may be read as that ongoing conversation. One only has to read the Psalms to see the variety of forms that conversation takes—praise, hard questions, complaints, puzzlement, lamentation, and expressions of awe and wonder. Because of our ability with language we are response-able. And we are *responsible* because we are *response-able*.

3. The Genesis story shows us that we are answerable, and it also shows us that we have a calling, in particular the calling to stewardship. We are called to be caretakers of the creator's world—a world God loves, a world in which God's glory is manifest.

4. The Genesis story also reveals that we humans are not satisfied with our creature/steward situation. We want to be the master, not the servant; we want to be the owner, not the steward; and we do not want to be accountable. We would rather deny and hide. We do not like having to live well within limits, practicing *shalom*. We want to set the agenda and master everything for our own wants.

5. The Genesis story makes clear to us that we are at the most fundamental level children of the same parents. We are, beneath our differences, brothers and sisters. This implies that difference is a surface phenomenon, not a deep one. All attempts to see the world in "us/them" ways tell only a fractional truth. We should be suspicious of all rhetoric that begins with this chauvinistic assumption.

A second biblical story, and the primary informing story for the Christian, is the story of God's love for the world manifest in Jesus. God comes into the world and embraces the world in love, being human to show us what being human is all about. The shocking thing about the story is that this embrace of the world finally takes the form of the cross. But the crucifixion, rather than being a tragic end, makes it possible for humans to realize a new life in Christ. We are transformed, new creatures, for Christ now lives in us as we embrace the world in love.

What follows from seeing Christ as the model of humanity?

1. It implies that things that are held to be of such great importance to the culture (wealth, status, political and military might, gender, ethnicity, being a religious insider/outsider) are worth very little.

2. It implies that we reach out to the outsider in need, that we are intentional boundary-crossers.

3. It implies that we practice a community that refracts God's love into the world in which we live.

The Christian image of the human is Christ. The Christian understanding of human relationship is *agape*, unconditional love. The Christian understanding of community is *koinonia*, a coming together that realizes the reign of God. The model of responsible human agency is *vocation*, a way of working that allows us to focus on the real needs of the neighbor. The human mode of being is *gifted freedom*. As Luther so clearly put it:

> A Christian is a perfectly free lord of all, subject to none. A Christian is a perfectly dutiful servant of all, subject to all. . . . Freed from the vain attempt to justify himself . . . [the Christian] should be guided by this thought alone . . . considering nothing but the need of the neighbor.

I believe that the story that informs our understanding of what it means to be human is one of the most important things that we learn in life. It is more important than the particulars that we learn and soon forget. It is more important because it shapes who we will become, how we understand ourselves, and what we will do (and not do) with the rest of the education we receive. When we honor our alumni we should ask more than, "What are their achievements? Are they a success as the culture counts success?" We should ask, "What kind of humans have they become? What message are we conveying to our students by honoring them?"

The Lutheran Contribution

What have Lutherans brought to the discussion of whole personhood? There are a few things. It is not that these things are exclusively Lutheran, but that Lutherans have emphasized them and have good historical and theological reason to emphasize them. Here is a short list:

Luther's understanding of *freedom*, mentioned above. Being freed from securing our own right relationship with God, we are free to attend to the needs of the world and our neighbor at hand. Lacking freedom we are all puppets of the powers that dominate our culture.

Engaged and caring criticism and self-criticism. Luther was certainly critical and self-critical, yet he was not critical the way a cynic is critical, dissociating himself from those things of which he is critical. Luther was most critical of the things he cared most about.

A skepticism about the division of the world into neat dualisms —sacred and secular, body, mind, and soul. Because of the Lutheran understanding of incarnation and sacrament, Lutherans tend to see the sacred *in* the secular, religious calling *in* everyday work, worship *in* everyday tasks, etc.

The deep appreciation and practice of music and other expressive and celebratory arts. Luther said that music was second in importance only to the word of God. It is clearly one of those places where flesh and spirit, thought and emotion come together in a most vivid way. Luther also saw God manifest in the everyday physical world, including his pint of beer and the gathering of friends at his table.

Seeing all work as vocation, an opportunity to share the love of God and one's own gifts by serving the real needs of the neighbor and the deep needs of the world.

Practicing paideutic education, i.e. education that integrates the acquisition of knowledge with the development of the student as a person. Unlike the prevailing model at most universities, professors at Lutheran colleges have been practicing paideutic education for generations.

How This Image of the Human Might Inform Education

I am not so deluded as to suppose that I will say the last word on this topic. I believe that "how do we educate for wholeness?" is one of those open questions that we never finish asking and reconsidering. So, what I do hope is to say something provocative, something that will begin or advance the discussion, not end it.

Toward the end of a faculty retreat that focused on education for whole personhood, I invited the participants to articulate what we hoped to be the product of our efforts at educating. Here is what we came up with. We want to educate a person who:

Is not just . . .	but is . . .
fitted with one skill or one domain of knowledge	broad, deep, and adaptable
a person with a diploma	a genuine learner
well-informed	an inquirer, part of a community of inquirers
a job holder	a person with a passion, a calling, a vocation
a person with an opinion	a critical thinker who gives and respects reasons
critical of others	capable of self-criticism, corrigible
a partisan	a partner in genuine dialogue
a strong mind	an open mind, capable of continued learning
a contact or acquaintance	a friend
a problem seer	a problem solver
an observer	a person actively engaged
an ego	a person connected in community and relationship
a cynic, a disconnected critic	a person who cares
a realist	a person with hope, willing to act on the change they desire for the world

Toward this end, education, informed by the biblical, Christian, and Lutheran understanding of the human, should include:

- The communication of awe, wonder, and thanksgiving in all the things we learn about the world, seeing it as a gift to be savored and shared, not just a bunch of resources to be selfishly used and wasted.

- The study and practice of creation stewardship—learning to live sustainably on this planet and respectfully with our fellow creatures. This is particularly difficult because there are no teachers; none of us are masters of this discipline, only learners.

- Criticism and self-criticism—learning to participate in a community that is free to consider any view and critique all those things in our culture that seem to demand absolute commitment. Such a community should be free, open, respectful, and appreciative of diversity. We should learn to criticize the things we care about, practicing criticism as a form of care.

- Be openly suspicious of all forms of chauvinism: nationalistic, racial, economic, cultural, ideological, *and* religious.

- Study and practice justice, peace-making, community building, victim solidarity.

- Vocational education—i.e. education that leads not just to a job or just down the path of a career, but rather that leads to an understanding of jobs and careers as a calling, a way, in love, that our gifts may intersect with the deep needs of the world.

- A chance to hear the biblical and Christian informing stories and weigh them over against the stories that dominate our culture and rule over so many of our lives.

- Education that connects to the deep questions, anxieties, and hopes that students have.

- Ample opportunities to participate in the arts including music, dance, theater, and the visual arts and the ways all these arts can be brought together in worship and the celebratory life of a college or university. Create liturgies of connection.

- Education that challenges over-simple either/ors and affirms both/ands.

- Education that challenges academic boundaries and fragmented views of reality.

- Education that unites theory and practice, academic learning and community engagement, reflection and life, analyzing serious problems and giving hope.

If we were to make wholeness a genuine academic end, we would have to be aware of the ways that academe undermines wholeness.

But more than just avoiding these things, we also need to work deliberately to counter them. We must:

- Challenge academic separations and the structures that support them.
- Deliberately unite theory and practice, academy, community, and world.
- Connect learning and experience and learning with personal development.
- Educate both for connected breadth and for depth.

As you can see this is not a curriculum, certainly not a list of courses, though it certainly could have curricular implications. Nor is it a pedagogy exactly, though it has implications for that as well. Rather it is the cement that holds the curricular bricks together, that relates the academic to the student services part of any college. It is an agenda for asking questions about what we consider to be the most important things we teach, require, and hope our students will do.

What is the end in light of which we choose educational means? Who is the human whom this education will shape? As a Christian college in the Lutheran tradition, do we take the biblical informing stories seriously? If so, where is that seriousness manifest? If we do not take them seriously, why not? Is it because we really serve the consumerist model of student success and life achievement? Or is it that, in spite of the lip service we may pay to a religious tradition, we do not take its image of the human seriously? If that is so, then religious language has also become a euphemism, a happy talk that means nothing. Or perhaps in spite of our Christian/Lutheran facade we really worship the pantheon of gods the culture advances—wealth, success, prestige, respectability, consumption, entertainment, and oblivion. That's a particularly deep failure for a religion like Christianity whose theology is informed by the challenging humanity of Jesus and the shocking and liberating good news of the presence of God's kingdom in the world.

Do Lutheran colleges and universities do well in the process of educating toward whole personhood? There is solid evidence that Lutheran colleges are quite good in many of these areas and not bad in others. But I am sure there are also some of these we do poorly and some not at all.

So, what should we do? I suggest these six priorities:

- Quit doing things in a particular way simply because that is the way everybody does them.
- Take the claim to be educating the whole person seriously.
- Make clear and explicit what the model of the whole human is toward which we educate.
- Explore the implications of the biblical/Christian/Lutheran model as well as solicit other models people may wish to put forward.
- Find educational means that actually lead to our educational ends.
- Quit being a cause of human fragmentation and narrowness, and start becoming part of the solution.

CHAPTER NINE

Responsible Knowing and the Loss of the Human

When I wrote *The Gift and Task of Lutheran Higher Education*, I was of the opinion that Chapters IV and V were the most important part of the book. They are the two chapters about the difficulties of relating faith and knowledge and about knowing responsibly. At one time I proposed that the title of the whole book should be *On the Outrageous Idea of a Lutheran Epistemology*. But those two chapters, it has turned out, are the least attended to and least discussed part of the book. It is as though we academics, constantly focused on the acquisition and dissemination of knowledge, just do not want to think about what we do or how we do it. It is assumed, perhaps, that the faith orientation of the university has something to do with chapel, the campus pastor, benedictions, etc., but nothing essentially to do with the inquiry and knowing that goes on there. But, unless I am extremely wrong about this, it is one of the most important discussions we can have. Perhaps these issues come too close to the heart of our identity as academics. Like the father in the film, *Moonstruck*, we moan over and over, "I don't want to think about it."

Knowledge as Achievement *and* Problem?

We often congratulate ourselves on how much more we know about the world than our ancestors did. There is an obvious sense in which that is true. But we often forget the other sides to this issue.

1. My father died in the mid-1950s when I was very young. But in spite of my youth I remember some things about him very vividly. He was not a highly educated man. In fact he had never graduated from high school. But in spite of his lack of schooling he had a great deal of practical knowledge. At the time he died he had only encountered one

thing that he could not understand the workings of and repair—that was a TV set. He repaired cars, electric motors, and radios. He did plumbing and electrical repairs. He maintained steam engines; he built houses and sea-going ships; he dug wells and designed windmills. He made spinning wheels and even built the lathe that he used for wood-turning. I finished high school and college and went on to get a Ph.D., but I do not know how to do any of those things. The point is that we may know things that our ancestors did not, but they also knew many things that we do not. Knowledge grows, but that growth is not necessarily cumulative.

2. As we learn new things, we also discover there are a host of things we do not know. It is as though the questions grow in direct proportion to our answers. As our telescopes have gotten more powerful, we have come to know stars and even galaxies of which we had no experience previously. But with that knowledge comes new questions: What explains the non-randomness of galactic clustering? Is the universe an incredible mass of matter, or does it also consist of some sort of negative matter? Is the universe expanding, or is space itself contracting? Do we have any way to tell the difference? Is the universe fundamentally orderly or chaotic? Is chaos a kind of order? Would we know chaos if we saw it?

We have come to know things about the human brain and nervous system that we never knew before we could do brain scans. We know that states of the brain profoundly influence our states of mind. Do states of mind also influence states of the brain? How is the vocabulary of consciousness related to the vocabulary of nerves, synapses, and brain matter? Will all my doubts, despair, anxieties, sorrows, and worries someday be ameliorated by swallowing a pill?

We know how to create herbicides, insecticides, and genetically altered species. What we do not know is what the ultimate consequence of their use may be. Are they responsible for the dramatic drop off in honey bee populations? Do the poisons finally enter the food chain only to increase the likelihood of human diseases or the incidence of conditions like autism or the sudden onset of allergies? The problem is that we do not know. Yet we use these things as though we knew they were harmless. We proceed with what my doctor calls "anxious confidence."

3. As our knowledge increases, so do the problems of knowing how to responsibly use that knowledge. Until we knew how to keep a body alive on a respirator and use artificial heart and kidneys, we never had the moral problem about "pulling the plug." Basically there was no plug to pull. Until we knew how to do organ transplants, we were not tempted to hasten the death of an accident victim to get his organs for someone else's use.

Back in the late 1960s I took part in a panel that addressed the question, "How should the government use its funds—to promote new scientific research or to use the knowledge we have to work on solvable problems?" Senator Walter Mondale was one of the panelists, and he brought two headlines from national newspapers—one announcing the first successful artificial heart transplant and one announcing that hundreds of thousands of Americans are malnourished. The latter problem we could solve with the knowledge we have; hundreds of thousands of persons would be made healthier. The former problem was an advance in knowledge costing millions to accomplish that, to that date, had helped only a handful. All the scientists on the panel thought that if we had to choose we should sink our money into new research. What argument would justify that choice, and what would its assumptions be?

Our new knowledge of genetics has increased both what we can do and increased our puzzlement about what it is appropriate to do. How far should we go with the creation of new species of plants and animals? Will we soon be able to predict the health of a child before it is born? Will we be able to "design" our own children? Will we be able to map the probabilities of our own health futures? Will we hire, insure, or marry people (or refuse to do these things) on the basis of this information? Will we be able to clone whole herds of animals for special purposes? Will we be able to create cloned sources for our own replacement body parts? A recent article in the local newspaper suggested cloning the 2008 Pittsburgh Steelers for another Super Bowl win twenty-five years in the future. It seems silly now, but will it always?

During World War I scientists developed poisonous gases they used as weapons. During World War II scientists developed nuclear weapons. During the Cold War scientists developed bombs that made the nuclear devices used during World War II look like toys. Chemists have discovered substances that are so poisonous that only a few drops in the water supply of a city would result in mass murder. Biologists have found viral weapons that dwarf the killing power of guns and bombs.

Scientists can do such things. More important than the question about our ability to do such things is the question about whether we ought to do them. Are we wise enough to have such knowledge? Are we, like the sorcerer's apprentice, clever enough to control nature but not wise enough to control ourselves?

No Place for the Human?

The era of modern science has seen the advance of knowledge through the mathematization and objectification of reality. Physics became the paradigm of knowing, so the more like physics our knowing could become the more scientific it was assumed to be. For many parts of reality we do not any longer have a language humans can speak. Reality is written in the language of mathematics. It is not a surprise then that most of us do not understand it. Nor is it a surprise that, when scientists try to talk about it to a lay audience, they speak in terms of occult forces and mysteries: black holes, dark matter, quarks, etc.

At one time people spoke about character, virtue, obligation, love, courage, and determination. In the early part of the twentieth century such language was pushed aside for talk about psychology, childhood trauma, biological urges, and sublimation. Now such language has been pushed aside in favor of a language of neuro-pharmacology. The farther our knowledge of ourselves goes, the less human we discover ourselves to be. Our story is the reverse of the Pinocchio story. Pinocchio, through a progression in effort and reflection and self knowledge, becomes more and more human. We, through a progression of scientific objectification, have become more and more like a complex machine. I sometimes tease my students by claiming that I do not believe in romantic love. "It is," I say, "simply a trick played on us by our glands." I usually do not have any trouble getting them to argue with me. The question now has become, is everything? Consciousness itself, many scientists insist, is simply an illusion worked by the complexities of the brain.

The classic film, *Blade Runner*, depicts a race of people who discover that they are not humans at all but extremely cleverly engineered androids. They have the epiphenomena of a human life—a memory, a collection of photos of their childhood and family, emotions, loves and fears, cares and concerns, even a poetic consciousness. But their tragedy is their dawning awareness that they are not really human. Is that film a kind of prophecy? Are those creatures us?

Contemporary philosopher E.M Adams expresses our situation thus:

> Our identity, our rationality, our norms and values, and our social institutions are no longer underwritten by our intellectual vision of humankind and the world. In disenchanting the world in our effort to gain mastery of it, we evicted ourselves. It is a world in which we knower-agents have no place. Our selfhood, indeed the whole human phenomenon, is rendered a dangler without a context that makes our lives meaningful and our existence intelligible. Faced with this absurdity, the dominant response has been to reprocess ourselves conceptually in such a way that we . . . will fit into the world as scientifically defined. But in doing so we deny our humanity.

The modern era has been characterized by the tendency to completely separate the "Can we?" questions from the "Ought we?" questions. Is that how it must be? Is there another way to model the relation of knowledge and responsibility?

About this fracture between human wisdom and the conclusions of the sciences, Ernest Gellner has written:

> When serious issues are at stake we want real knowledge [scientific knowledge] . . . or at least what passes for scientific knowledge [conclusions sufficiently quantified]. . . . The price of real knowledge is that our identities, freedom, norms, and institutions are no longer underwritten by the vision and comprehension of things. On the contrary we are doomed to suffer from the tension between cognition and identity.

Knowledge for What? Educating for What?

I have many colleagues who resent my even asking, "What is knowledge for?" The assumption is that knowledge is good for its own sake, and the more of it the better. Maybe. But I am not completely convinced.

Aristotle maintained that humans had an essential human nature and that knowing—at least knowing that leads to understanding—is a fulfillment of our species nature. We thrive as human beings when we employ our rational powers. We achieve human well-being through knowing and understanding. Not many people make that argument anymore. Not many people believe there is an essential human nature. My students, at least most of them, are amused by Aristotle's assertion that in inquiry and study lies the greatest and most complete happiness.

It never occurred to Aristotle that the purpose of knowledge was to give humans mastery and control. That idea became dominant with the rise of science that focused on discovering causes and developing technology that gave us mastery over nature. That paradigm is still with us, but it does not have quite the power it once had.

About a decade ago I heard a lecture by a person who claimed that scientific knowledge had been doubling every seven years since the mid 1960s. When I asked him how he had calculated that, he responded that this was the rate of increase of published scientific papers. There is an interesting assumption at work there that he had neither recognized nor bothered to question. Is published research really a good measure of increases in knowledge? What that speaker had revealed was a new paradigm: We live in an age where the results of research, whether or not one counts these as advances in knowledge, are valued as currency in the academic game. The question is not, "Have we come to understand more?" nor even, "Have we learned something that will help us master nature?" The question seems to be, "Will this get me tenure or a promotion?" In the pursuit of success in this game, we have accumulated incredible amounts of information, stored in ever-increasing on-line or in-print journals. There are many too many for any person to keep up with even if one restricts one's reading to other scholars in one's sub-sub-discipline.

A miser is a person who collects money, not to spend it nor invest it, but to possess it. We seem to have become misers of academic knowledge. We create it and collect it in order to have it, to have our name connected with it, to run our mental fingers through it, perhaps even to recite it occasionally to an appreciative (or about to be tested) audience.

Many decades ago a St. Olaf College alumnus told me about a professor from the first half of the twentieth century who kept data of all sorts: the number of steps from his office to his regular seat in chapel, the number of times in a year that he climbed the stairs, absences in his class arranged by alphabet and by ethnic heritage and religious denomination, body proportions of adult men and women by ethnic grouping. At the end of each year he wrote up and published his findings. He also spoke in chapel the last day of each year, and his message was to read aloud all the verses of hymns that had been skipped during the academic year. This sounds like a fabrication, I know, but other St. Olaf alumni have verified these things for me.

We are amused by such an account not because it is untypical of college professors, but because we believe the data he collected so passionately and in such a disciplined way was trivial. But trivial by whose standards? Many years ago my wife got cornered at a faculty gathering by a professor who insisted on telling her about the accomplishments of generals in the War of 1812. I heard her respond in as cheery voice as she could muster, "Oh, a trivia expert." He lowered both his voice and his eyebrows and replied, "No, madame, that's called history."

Not long ago I heard on National Public Radio a description of a particular kind of autism called Asperger's Syndrome. I listened intently to the description. People who have it have an extremely passionate, well-developed cognitive mastery over a very small range of information. They also have trouble relating socially to others except when they find others who are interested in this same domain, and they cannot understand why everyone isn't passionately interested in their specialty. As I listened to this description I shouted, "That's not a description of autism; that's a description of college faculty!"

Are there other, and better, paradigms? I would like to suggest two, both of which are congruent with a Christian and Lutheran outlook:

1. We pursue knowledge as a way of celebrating the wonder and awe we feel in the presence of the complexities of creation. Luther somewhere wrote, "How could we not want to know about the wonders of creation?" The implication seems to be that to behold the creation without wonder, or to confront it in boredom, is a kind of blasphemy. It is like receiving a gift and not bothering to open it.

2. We pursue knowledge as a way to learn how to serve. Knowledge translates care into service. I may want to relieve the suffering of

a diseased person. Without knowledge I am not able to do so. I may want to live sustainably, but without knowledge I do not know what to do. I may want to provide good advice to a friend. Without knowledge I may misunderstand the problem or, worse, contribute to it.

We teach subjects, we teach modes of inquiry, but we also teach students. As I teach I have to maintain that double vision, carrying a responsibility to what I teach, but also a responsibility for whom I teach. As a consequence we must perennially quiz ourselves to see that we know the "what" of our teaching. But we also need to ask, "*Who* is the human that this process is aimed at developing, enabling, and encouraging?"

H.G. Wells, in his novel, *The First Men in the Moon*, has his lunar explorer report on the variety of lunar creatures. They all belong to a single species, but each has been modified to fit its task in life. In each some single organ has been developed at the expense of the others. The lunar explorer tells us:

> Quite recently I came upon a number of young Selenites confined in jars from which only their forelimbs protruded, who were being compressed to become machine minders of a special sort. The extended "hand" in this highly developed system of education . . . is nourished by injection while the rest of the body is starved . . . . It is unreasonable, I know, but such educational methods of these beings affect me most disagreeably. . . . It haunts me still, although it is really in the end a far more humane proceeding than our earthly method of leaving children to grow into human beings and then making machines of them.

Do we dare say that education is for whole personhood? For a life of responsible freedom? For a life of wonder-aliveness? For a life of stewardship and service? Is there a way to connect knowing and wisdom? Is there a way of knowing a world large enough to live in and a way of knowing appropriate for a human capable of meaningful life?

Learning and Teaching in a Lutheran University

A Lutheran university ought to be a place where such hard questions are taken seriously. In fact, it should be a place where such questions are central and perennially revisited. Knowledge and rightness, the combination that previous generations referred to as wisdom, should once again be focal. This should be so even if the wisdom that we acquire is to admit that we do not know how to handle our own cleverness. More than that, wisdom ought to be focal precisely because we are not wise, because we are frequently clever beyond our own good, because we can be so dangerous in our cleverness to both ourselves and the planet.

But how, then, should learning proceed in a Lutheran university?

1. Learning in a Lutheran university does not mean that we know by some special gift or technique not available to everyone else. I do not believe there is such a thing as Christian knowing or Lutheran knowing that gives us an advantage or superior insight into the nature of things. Some reformers said things like that, but Luther never did. He seemed to be aware that redemption and sanctification do not automatically bring intelligence or wisdom. A foolish Christian was as much a reality for Luther as a sinful Christian was. When we set out to know, we have to inquire in the same fallible ways as everyone else.

2. Learning in a Lutheran university does not imply that we should turn a blind eye to certain subjects, viewpoints, or theories on the grounds that they are too dangerous to think about. When I was a student at Concordia College, a well-meaning librarian cautioned me against reading too many of the works of Friedrich Nietzsche. "There are some ideas better left alone," she said. Since chemistry, biology, and physics can be used destructively, is it better not to know them? Should I try to persuade my daughter not to study neuro-science? Not at all. The solution is not to become an epistemological Luddite, to destroy laboratories, or smash all the microscopes. Nor is it to silence or censor the sciences. One trial of Galileo was too many.

3. Learning in a Lutheran university does mean that the sciences and every other subject should be pursued in a community of open inquiry. This inquiry should turn its attention to evidences for and against the theories advanced and also turn attention to both the assumptions and the implications of things we know and our ways of knowing them.

4. Learning in a Lutheran university also means that the pursuit of knowledge is interwoven with concern and care. In medicine the care is for patients and both the quality and quantity of life. In the earth sciences the care is for the environment and the species that are a part of it. In the social sciences the care is for persons, families, societies, cultures,

and economies. In the law the care is for justice and order. Learning in a Lutheran university weaves together concerns about truth with concerns about values. These concerns may well lead us in different directions, but that is a necessity in weaving. The threads cannot all be parallel. Allow me another analogy: Concern for truth is the wind that lifts the kite. But concern for the good and the just and the right, concern for essential values, is the string which holds it in check. The wind and the string will seem like they are at battle with each other. But if the string is cut, the kite comes down in a chaotic spiral. The flight of the kite is a tension between forces, but a productive one.

Someone might object that knowing should not be connected to any care, concern, or value. "Knowledge ought to be value-free," they say. Frankly, I am very suspicious of such so-called "value-free" inquiries. If inquiries do not serve real needs they almost always serve some kind of idol or other: wealth, power, the market, mastery, prestige, winning points in some academic game, etc. Inquiry that serves the needs of our neighbor, our patient, our client, the community, and the world—that seems far preferable to the service of those other values which we pretend are not there.

A Lutheran university should be, therefore, a place of lively dialogue, a place where people make and critique arguments, a place where diverse voices are heard and diverse concerns are expressed. The depth and liveliness of the dialogue ought to be one of the ways we measure our success. It ought to be what business folk call a KPI, an annual key performance indicator. The people we graduate should all have experienced the dialogue that should be a continuing part of their professional lives. People who go into business should be aware of the responsibility and interdependence of employers and employees, manufacturers and consumers, and businesses and the communities on which they depend. People who go into law should be aware of the tensions that the practice of law embodies. They should be aware of the ways in which the interest of attorneys and the interests of their clients may conflict, the ways that the legal system serves and sometimes fails to serve the needs of those who come to it in need. People in education should be aware of the good and the harm that can be worked in school. They should be critical and self-critical practitioners. They should be reflective professionals. They should be multi-dimensional humans as well as specialists.

In Chapter V of *The Gift and Task of Lutheran Higher Education*, "Toward a Lutheran Epistemology," I designate eight "epistemic principles," things that ought to characterize knowing in a Lutheran university, I repeat them here in the hope that someone may notice them this time around who did not attend to them before.

Knowing, in our colleges and universities, should be characterized by:

Wonder—openness to reality that does not fit into our ready-made conceptual boxes.

Openness—willingness to consider views and arguments from other points of view. A willingness to look through Galileo's telescope and actually consider Darwin's argument.

Recognition of connectedness—considering the essential relatedness of things that our university structure or curriculum may have completely separated.

Freedom—openness to consider any topic, any author, any theory. Frequently students say, "everyone's entitled to an opinion." I respond, "No, everyone is entitled to make an argument."

Critical faithfulness—willingness to be critical about things we care about. Criticism is not an act of betrayal but may be an act of deep love.

Engaged suspiciousness—suspicious concern for the motivations that stand behind our ways of seeing, our ways of inquiring, our so-called objectivity.

Vocation—diligence in asking, "Whom and how does this serve?"

Hope—persistence in the inquiry even when we fail to find an answer or we fail to resolve the tensions we have found. Tensions may be the reality at the basis of what we are studying. Or, as Goya wrote on the charcoal sketch of himself he did in his nineties, "I am still learning."

This discussion certainly does not close the subject. My point is once again to raise the questions: What does responsible knowing look like? How are our knowing selves related to our acting selves? Is the self that is known the same as the self that knows? What are the deep assumptions on which inquiry, knowing, and the sharing of knowledge rest?

The Real Needs of Students

I have described the vocation of a Lutheran college/university as meeting the real needs of students so that through their education they can serve the deep needs of the world. Earlier we focused our attention on the needs of the world and the types of persons the world needs to meet those needs, but we spent little time talking about the real needs of students. I turn now to that topic.

My Daughter's College Search

I traveled with my high school-age daughter to look at some colleges she thought she might want to attend. We visited seven. She evaluated them by what, at first, were a set of unarticulated criteria. Little by little she made explicit what those criteria were—to me, but more importantly, to herself: Did the school have the majors she wants? Did it have a good reputation particularly in those areas of interest to her? Was it academically demanding (though she wanted some time for music, theater, dance, and some goofing off)? Were the students serious about learning without being too geeky? Did they seem to enjoy each other? What were conversations like in the cafeteria, coffee shop, or other campus clusters? Did they have good science labs? Were there opportunities for student research? Were the dorms livable? Were there any cute boys? What was the area like? Could she imagine enjoying a weekend outing in the area or a Sunday walk in the campus environs?

The problem, of course, was that the place that was most academically demanding did not do well in the cute boy ranking, and the one that had the best reputation in her major did not seem to have a lively, happy community. The one with the prettiest campus did not have Mt. Ranier in the background. Through all these visits my daughter had a first-hand, if limited, experience of these seven colleges. So, did she find the best place?

The most important thing that happened in this process was the way she began to know herself. She had to examine her implicit criteria of evaluation and make them explicit. In so doing she also had a chance to critique them and to critique her own ability to judge them. She looked at college rankings, but she also came to recognize that they too had criteria, and that theirs and hers were not always the same. But most importantly, I think, she came to realize that the quality of the college as a place of learning would depend more on her than it would on the place. So the college search process became less like a shopping excursion and more like an exercise in personal reflection.

I tried to be a help to her in that process—by asking some questions, by questioning some answers, by reminding her that college is not graduate school and that most students change their majors somewhere along the way, by telling a few stories about my own college years, but most of all by keeping quiet and listening.

Those college visits also provided an opportunity for me to reflect about what I hoped for my daughter's college years. One step away was a reflection on what I should do for my students. Teachers are hired because of what they know and can communicate clearly and understandably to students. It helps if the teacher also loves or at least has some enthusiasm for his/her subject. Where that is absent or has been lost, learning can still take place, but it is an uphill climb. It also helps if the teacher is a continuing learner—continuing to inquire in the areas he/she teaches. In that situation the student learns the adventure of inquiry—which is, I believe, more valuable than just learning what the teacher knows. But there are other ways that college students can grow besides learning subjects and learning to inquire.

Real Needs: A Reflection

For students, college should include or be:

1. A community of persons who treat students as more than customers and commodities. There should be teachers and advisors who show some interest in each student as a "who" and not just a "what."

2. Some people who take students more seriously than they take themselves, who challenge them to perform beyond what anyone (including the students) think they are capable of doing. Examples: A choir director who in one year transforms a choir from mediocrity to excellence. A basketball coach who does the same. A teacher who says,

"I can't write you a recommendation until I have seen the best work of which you are capable." Another who says, "If you were running a race would you only run half as fast as you could? Why do you put so little effort into learning?"

3. A community of discipline. Students learn to be self-disciplined through practicing disciplines pressed on them by teachers, coaches, the peer group. Examples include sports teams, musical ensembles, study groups, class assignments with deadlines and consequences, theater involvement. Every college has assignments, but discipline is more a matter of campus culture than just a place of requirements.

4. An invitation to participate in a critical community of discourse. Examples include a student debating society, public forums for the discussion of difficult issues, symposia where students have their research displayed and critiqued, student recitals where students show what they can do and what they still have to learn.

5. An invitation to begin a life-long conversation with significant minds—an encounter with the thinking of Plato and Aristotle, the teachings of Jesus and the Buddha, the vision of Rembrandt and Rothko, the characters of Dostoevsky and Wolfe. A life is rich in proportion to the conversations it has.

6. A sense of presence. College prepares students for work that comes after and a world beyond the ivy wall, so in many things there will be this "after this" or "over there" reference. But a good college also has a sense of being in the present. There should also be a realization of what a lively, dynamic, exciting community is like and what life in it could be: plays, concerts, games, late night conversations, excellent friendships, opportunities for gathering as congregation, small groups as well as solitude.

7. Earned self-confidence. Self-confidence does not come from never being challenged or criticized. It comes from doing well at a task that the student respects. It is a saying to oneself, "I think I can do this, because I have done things like this in the past."

8. All of the above are necessary conditions for the realization of freedom. A most misunderstood conception in our culture, freedom is in some respects the most valuable and the most difficult goal of human becoming. We seem to believe in our culture that freedom is being able to make choices. If that were so we would be most free when we

are in the cereal aisle of the grocery. I would say freedom is more like respecting and trusting the self that chooses. An addict is not free no matter how many choices he is given. A person who lives in fear is not free either. I may have many choices, but if the choice I finally make is not *mine*, if it does not connect with my real identity, I am not free. I am simply somebody's puppet. It matters little that the strings are connected to my mind rather than my limbs.

Isn't all education an education toward freedom? Unfortunately not, I'm afraid. A good part of what passes for education is a kind of training for a life of slavery of one sort or another. Ralph Waldo Emerson in his famous essay, "Self Reliance," talks about learning to speak authentically in the first person, to be able to say, "I think, I am, I desire, I hope." He describes a fulfilled life as "becoming a self it is mine to become on behalf of a world it is mine to desire." What is the world that students desire? Do they know? Do they know how to think their way through to an answer, or do they await the next issue of *Vogue*, *GQ*, or *Auto World* to inform them?

It is always nice when a student leaves college who has a job. But so much better and more exciting is the student who leaves with a knowledge of who they are, with a vision of life and the world that excites them, with a passion, a sense of calling. My two oldest daughters both quit jobs they got soon after college graduation. They quit because they discovered that their employer was cheating his customers, and they refused to be part of the scam. I was proud of their unemployment.

All the things in the above list are connected. Every student (every person) needs to have experienced the discipline, the critical reflection borne out of practice and dialogue to know and trust their own self. Only then is freedom a possibility.

Can my youngest daughter or I tell whether a college will address or meet those needs? It is not in the curriculum, in the campus or facilities, or in the fame or credentials of the faculty. I would say it lies in the culture, in the humanity of the faculty and in the character of the student community. This is very hard to detect on a short visit. Selecting a college is largely an act of faith. You can tell if it is the right place only by watching to see what kind of person one becomes by being there for a while. It can be detected, it can be seen, but it takes time and trust to find it. When it occurs it is a wonder and a delight—and, I suppose, something of an everyday miracle.

CHAPTER ELEVEN

Shaping the Culture of a College

When I was taking my youngest daughter to visit colleges to which she might apply, I tried to pay attention to the criteria that she was employing in making her decisions. She had already done a good deal of sorting. She had made a list of seven schools she wanted to visit. They were all fairly small liberal arts colleges. They all had strong reputations in science and math as well as other subjects. They all encouraged a pattern of education valuing breadth as well as depth. So, when we visited these seven colleges, what were we looking for? My daughter would have said that she wanted to know what *the people* were like—faculty, staff, and students—what *the place* was like—campus, location, and architecture—and finally what *the college character* was like—vision, identity, and values. I would have said we were looking at *institutional culture*.

If I had to characterize the culture of my alma mater, Concordia College in Moorhead back in the 1960s, I would say that it was clearly Lutheran (mostly Lutheran students, mostly Lutheran faculty, mostly Lutheran administrators), that it was midwestern provincial (students from farms and small towns in Minnesota and the Dakotas plus a few Montanans and Canadians), that it was middle class, that it was pervaded by a Norwegian-American ethos (holiday food, pietist values, Norwegian sweaters for sale in the book store), and that it preserved and celebrated the Lutheran choral tradition and a kind of home-grown tradition in the visual arts. Some of those elements are still there, but some of them have changed pretty radically. Concordia, like almost all Lutheran colleges, was trying to work out a kind of tension in its identity. It was a college founded by immigrants to educate a new generation in a way that both preserved the immigrant traditions and values, and prepared people to do well in a new world. Of necessity it was a college trying to preserve an old legacy *and* shape a new world.

Some colleges still preserve an ethnic identity, a rural identity, and a singular religious identity. Many others have found themselves serving in a much more urban and more ethnically and religiously diverse world. Their vision, identity, and values will naturally have changed. Who would have supposed that Concordia would become nationally recognized for its programs of global outreach and language study as well as for its choir and department of religious studies? Who would have imagined forty years ago that Augsburg College would be noted for the way it has embraced the city of Minneapolis or for the ways it has come to serve the Native American, Latino, and Somali populations in its neighborhood?

For the present I will focus on three main topics: the culture of active learning, the double message of general education, and the culture of faculty scholarship. I choose these three because each designates a particular problem, a particular complaint, that is common to many colleges I have recently visited as well as colleges where I have served. You may find that some of the topics discussed here are not problems at your college. On the other hand they may be problems that you had not really noticed.

The Culture of Active Learning

Complaint: The vast majority of students who come to our college are not active learners. They study a foreign language because it is required; they do what is necessary to get by but no more than that; and they learn enough to pass the exam, pass the course, and get the degree or certificate. The point of college for them is that piece of paper, that signal that they are finally done. The point of college is, for them, to be done with learning, not to continue it; to do the minimum that is required, not the maximum.

Analysis: I heard a student bragging to his buddies about how little work he had managed to do during the past semester: "I did none of the reading, skipped about half the classes, and got my girlfriend to write the two essays that were required. Still I passed the class. I sure put one over on them, didn't I? Isn't that cool?"

Now imagine this analogous comment: "I bought a year's membership to this new fitness club. But—guess what— I only went there six times, and I never worked out enough to break a sweat. I sure pulled a fast one on them. Isn't that cool?" And another: "I spent sixty dollars at the super market. I loaded up the cart, checked out all the stuff, got the receipt, and then left the groceries right there in the cart. I sure put one over on them. Isn't that cool?"

My guess is that the attitude expressed in the first example is very common. The attitude expressed in the second also is fairly common. (One of my former students is the manager of a health club and tells me that they always admit about twice as many members as they can hold, knowing that more than half will never show up.) But I suppose that the third example never happens.

My question is this: Why is it not as obvious in the first two cases that the person is paying the bill but leaving without the groceries? Why, in particular, do so many people not see that the person who has been fooled in this instance is not some alien "them" but the enrollee himself? The reason, I believe, is because there are three notions that are deeply embedded in our culture:

1. We are quick to identify the end or purpose of the activity with the certificate or degree obtained, rather than with the change that occurs to the participant. It is as if I got a four-year certificate for attendance at a weight loss program but never, in the process, lost any weight nor changed my eating patterns. Or it is as if I "took" two years of Spanish—I can show you my transcript—but I cannot speak or read the language.

2. We are used to believing that education is something purchased in consumable units. We sometimes ask, "Where did you get your education?" just like we would ask, "Where did you buy that nice tie?" We are always on the lookout for a good deal, so we want to get the maximum schooling credits for the minimum cost. And the huge assumption we make is that the effort of studying and learning is part of the cost.

3. We are quick to assume that education is something we do because someone else requires it, not because we desire it. The school board required that we go to elementary and high school, our mom required that we take piano and dance lessons, the state and the school mandated certain requirements so we "had to take" algebra and American history and so many units of physical education. We never did any of this because we wanted to learn it, because we desired it, or because we wanted to be transformed by it. Thus when I ask first-year college

students to make an inventory of things they want to learn while they are in college, most of them stare at me as though I were from some other galaxy. Occasionally one will answer something that has nothing to do with college, such as, "I've thought of learning to play the banjo," but it is extremely rare for a student to see college as a vast opportunity for their own learning, growth, or transformation. When we do meet the rare student who wants to learn more, or more widely or more deeply, we think some kind of miracle has occurred.

This general condition is what philosophers have called alienation. It is what happens when something that naturally belongs to us has been given or taken away by some institution. This is why patients often do not follow the therapies recommended by their doctors. This is why we pass laws and hire police to enforce them while we secretly plan to avoid them. This is why people quickly gain back the weight lost once the weight loss program has ended. This is why we minimize our own efforts at learning and are happy to forget anything we have learned once the school year has ended.

Why would we not want to learn as much as possible, as well and as deeply as possible? Why would I want to learn Spanish in a half-hearted way when I could (for the same cost) learn it well? I believe the answer is that we have been schooled by our culture to be alienated from our own improvement. Can we now be un-schooled or re-schooled to become active, self-motivated, continuing learners?

Strategies for change: I am not at all sure that this problem can be eliminated. It is too deep seated in the whole schooling culture to which we have been exposed since kindergarten, but there are some things we can and should do to make things better. All three of these suggestions have to do with beginning to change the culture:

1. We must identify this cultural assumption and make it clear to everyone—to every faculty member hired, to every administrator and staff person, to every student who sets foot on our campus, and to every parent of every student. We cannot address the problem if we do not recognize it, just like we cannot avoid a fallacy if we cannot identify it. All the view books and mailers we send out must recognize the temptation and the cultural habit of thinking about education as something passively received by students and required by society or the institution.

2. We must replace such language and such ideas with a different way of thinking, talking, and behaving. The primary agent of education is the student. Faculty are resources for student learning. The activities of students will result in learning, not the activities of faculty. The primary activities of education are reading, discussing, conversing, exercising, writing, editing, exploring, experimenting, and practicing. These are activities the student will be doing. The student who sits idly by to watch the activity of the teacher is not learning very much, if anything. I cannot get better at tennis by watching the pros play the game on TV. I cannot get better at playing the cello by listening to Yo-Yo Ma recordings. I cannot become a better essayist just by reading someone else's work.

Faculty can join in the activities of learning. They can model learning, and they can coach learning. Faculty always must be aware that learning is seldom the result of teaching. Last year a fellow faculty member was alarmed when he found out how little his students had actually learned. His response was, "Well, then, I must teach them more and teach them harder." Someone needed to point out the huge assumption at work there and suggest an alternative way to come at this. Will adding five minutes of lecture time to each class result in a ten percent increase in learning? I doubt it will make any appreciable difference.

We must be careful about what we say. We must challenge each others' ways of speaking and thinking. When a student says, "*You* gave me a C for the course," we must respond, "*I* didn't give you anything. Here's the amount and the quality of work you did." We should replace teacher-active verbs with student-active ones. A syllabus should be an agenda of student activities, not an agenda of the teacher's activities. If I say, "I taught logic last semester to twenty-two students," someone should suggest instead that I say, "Twenty-two students studied and practiced logic last semester, and I coached them."

3. When we welcome new students onto our campus, we should put in front of them the work of our accomplished seniors and recent graduates. We should say, "Here's what we expect you will be able to do in a little while if you work at it. We expect you'll be able to do biology research as well as Wendy. We expect that you'll be able to do a violin recital as fine as Hunter's. We expect you'll be able to write a short story as good as Eliot's. We expect you'll be able to construct an

entrepreneurial business model as exciting as Isabel's. Do you want to be able to do that? We believe you can."

By doing this we will be setting a high standard. We will be showing what kind of growth and development is possible, and, in each case, we will be doing this by showing what students have done. This helps, from the outset, to establish a culture of active student learning.

The Culture of General Education

Complaint: It is not uncommon that colleges are of two minds about general education or the core curriculum. On the one hand we think these studies are so important that everyone must do them regardless of major or program; on the other hand we staff over half the sections with adjunct faculty. Are these studies a priority or not? On the one hand we make these studies the center of our curriculum; on the other hand we disvalue them and talk about them disparagingly both to our colleagues and our students. We often talk about them as "courses to get out of the way," so important work can be done.

Students pick up quickly on this double-speak and are confused by it. Are these studies important or trivial, foundational or tangential? Are they the least important of our studies or the most important, something to be avoided if possible (by both faculty and students) or absolutely essential? If we as faculty and administrators are not clear and consistent about this, then how in the world can we expect that students will understand?

Analysis: Given what we said previously about promoting a culture of active learning, is there something wrong with the whole idea of general education *requirements*? Do they take us back to a passive and alienated model of learning? Do they say to the student, "We really don't trust you with your own education, so we will tell you what you must learn"?

To some degree the college makes decisions for its students by the curriculum it offers. There are schools in Ohio where you can learn to drive a sixteen-wheeler; there is a university in Texas where you can get a major in baton twirling. The college where I teach does not offer either. Nor do we have offerings in weaving, textile design, Norwegian, Italian, or playing the accordion. It is not that we have decided that these things are not worth learning, though I would argue that some of them do not belong in a college curriculum. It is that we just do not have the resources to offer everything.

Or do we? Since Capital University is located in a large city (fifteenth largest in the country), it could become a broker for learning in all of the above areas, a place where a group of students with an interest in learning Polish can connect with persons capable of speaking it. A college could be a learning network, loosely structured to allow for the maximum flexibility. So by next spring we could have groups studying Polish, managerial accounting, the films of Ingmar Bergmann, Sufism, and beginning hurdy-gurdy. This might be valuable. We could truly rename ourselves, All Things to All People U. What we would not have is a coherent community with a single informing vision of what education is or what an educated person in this day and age should look like.

I do not want my examples to convey the impression that I think such things are not worth learning. If a child of mine had told me of her interest in any of these things, I like to think I would encourage and support her efforts to learn them. The question before us is: Are all of these appropriate collegiate foci of study? Are they all appropriate studies for a small liberal arts college? Are they appropriate studies for a Christian college that is informed by the Lutheran concepts of grace, freedom, critical reflection, stewardship, and vocation? Even more to the point, are they *essential* studies for students enrolled in such a place? Now here, I believe, we have a place to begin again the conversation about an essential core of learning at our college. This conversation can be fruitful because we have decided not to try to be all things to all people and because we have decided not to be a Walmart University, offering a merely generic curriculum with a generic faculty. So the mere existence of a college or university like ours poses a question to prospective students and to the culture: Who needs a Lutheran college? Would All Things to All People U or Generic U not serve just as well? I believe that the answer is no. I believe that only an institution that has a clear image of the human who is being educated has the right to offer a core curriculum that is more than a mere cafeteria of selections. Only such institutions can answer the questions: "Why is this essential? Why this and not that?"

Strategies for change:

1. We should always embed our discussions of curriculum within our explanations of our mission, vision, and values. Apart from such explanations, the discussions of core curriculum seem arbitrary and

disconnected. In the context of an institution shaped by the Lutheran understanding of grace, stewardship, freedom, critical reflection, and vocation, discussions of curriculum are answers to questions such as these: What do we have to learn to be good stewards? To be free? To be critically engaged? To serve well the deep needs of the world? To realize our giftedness? Without such a context, courses will remain just an arbitrary, alien requirement. Within such a context, the curriculum is intimately connected to the questions: Who am I? What am I called to be?

2. Students should be regularly asked to write or revise their own educational philosophy, articulating the ends and means of learning and their connection to the human they intend to be. Advising should be a critical conversation about what the student has stated, pointing out assumptions made, alternatives to be considered, etc. Unfortunately often, advising is merely a way of registering a student for requirements, and it is neither critical nor reflective nor connected in any essential way to the student's own agenda for learning.

3. If there are studies that are closely connected to the vision and values of the college, they should be staffed with people who are very clear about that connection. If these things are important and essential, then they deserve the best care that we can give them. That may mean assigning our tenured faculty to these studies, or it may not. It may mean that we give particular attention to educate faculty to do this work. It should not mean just sticking in some random person, called "generic staff," to do the job. If the college and the faculty give these studies their best attention, the probability that the students will do so is also increased.

The Culture of Faculty Scholarship

Complaint: Most colleges want to encourage faculty scholarship. Many make it a significant criterion for evaluation for tenure or promotion. In the past three years I have become well acquainted with three colleges fitting that latter description. Interestingly, all three have had some difficulty defining evaluation rubrics for faculty scholarship. Scholarship can, after all, look very different in different disciplines. What passes for scholarship in chemistry is usually very different from scholarship in history. Both are different from the scholar's activity in musical performance or theater. Thus the first problem is comparing scholarly activities across disciplines.

What do we do when the activity of a faculty member falls outside of or is tangential to the area in which the person teaches? What do we do with the fact that a professor of psychology publishes three short stories? Do these count as his scholarly accomplishments? Or what happens when a Luther scholar develops a passion for Sri-Lankan Buddhist art and becomes one of the world's leading lecturers on the subject? Or what happens when a professor of music becomes excited by the fiction of Milan Kundera and reads everything he ever wrote? Is this a project worthy of sabbatical support? What do we do when a professor of political science submits three thousand photographs of war refugees taken in Africa in support of her promotion? What do we say to a professor who wants to use his sabbatical to learn Finnish and Estonian? Should such things count as scholarship? These examples are not fictions, and each raises a real problem.

Analysis: One of the easy answers to the question is to stipulate that scholarship is defined within the bounds of a discipline. Philosophy is what appears in philosophy journals, economics is what people do who read papers at economists' conventions, etc. A second easy answer is to say that something counts as scholarship only if it is directly connected to fulfilling one's job description. What does reading Kundera have to do with teaching music theory? What does Sri Lankan art have to do with teaching a class on the Reformation? If one were teaching creative writing, then publishing short stories would count, but if one teaches criminal and introductory psychology, then it does not. These are easy answers because they are ways of avoiding the problem. I, however, do not find them satisfying.

I think that we have to step back a bit and ask ourselves a series of hard and deep questions: What is the academic community we are striving to develop? What kind of persons are we hoping this community will grow? What kind of learning do we hope faculty will model? What kind of learning must faculty have and maintain in order to do their jobs well? I think that if we press these questions with diligence we will discover that there is not a single or simple answer that emerges. Learning can and does take a variety of forms.

On the edge of the campus where I teach is a sign that occasionally says, "Capital University, A Community of Learners." I am always happy to see that sign because it gives me a sense of belonging. My favorite definition of a teacher is, "a communicative learner." By that definition, of course, many of our students are teachers. All of our teachers should also be students. In a learning-focused community the fact that we cannot easily tell the difference should not be a problem, but an occasion for pride.

Strategies for change:

1. We need to engage the entire community, including the board of trustees, in a discussion of the hard and deep questions raised above. Some people seem to believe that we can address such questions without reference to the institution's mission, vision, and values. I do not see how that is possible. What kind of community of learners do we wish to be? Are there some kinds of continued learning that are essential, while others are good but tangential? Where is the center of the circle from which that measurement is taken?

2. We need to explicate our community's understanding of valued scholarship. We need to make it exceptionally clear where and how our standards of evaluation differ from those dominant in the graduate school academic culture. Many graduate programs make it clear they are looking for "original research." Many institutions expand that to mean "original research that attracts research grant money." A former colleague of mine in philosophy was led by the demand for original research to a dissertation topic on some little-known eighteenth century Swedish thinker. He honestly had little interest in the ideas or the works of this man. He would rather have been working on reading and understanding the works of Heidegger. But hundreds of dissertations had been written on Heidegger while none, to his knowledge, had ever been written on the work of Nikolai Sils Hedlund. Thus this demand for originality drove him away from the deep and interesting, toward the dull and trivial. A colleague in political science, driven by the demand that his research be quantitative, spent years sorting data to prove the thesis, "The foreign policy of small European nations is influenced by the foreign policy of large European nations." My reaction, and his own, was, "Well, duh." The work, accompanied by 230 pages of computerized data, got him a publication and tenure. A third example is the work of a current colleague whose research proved the thesis, "Bacteria levels in underwear are directly proportional to length of wear." This research was funded by a grant from the U.S. Navy and supervised by the National Science Foundation. It is no wonder that many faculty refer to such endeavors as "playing the graduate

school game." But it has also become the "getting your work published game." No one that I know particularly likes it, although some who get good at it have learned to play it to their profit. Is this the game we want our faculty to play and play well? We must have the courage to have that conversation and, I think, to question that paradigm.

3. If we are going after different paradigms, we must make it clear what they are and how they will work in practice. Let me suggest three:

a. Give priority of place to scholarship that is connected to the desired learning outcomes of students. If my students are heading out to be health care professionals in Northern Minnesota and Wisconsin, then I would do well to know the particular health care needs of the people who live there. If my students are interested in becoming journalists, then I should know how drastically that profession has changed in the last decade. If my students are interested in child psychology, then I had better know what the recent research is related to that field. If I am helping to prepare students to enter the business world, then I had better know how new communications media have changed the way business is done. What does it mean to work in a global marketplace? If the last time I worked in the marketplace was thirty years ago, I am probably hopelessly out of date.

b. If we are educational institutions that take Luther's idea of vocation seriously, then we will want to give priority of place to scholarship that is connected to meeting the deep needs of the world we are called to serve. Many of the examples given above do that. What do I need to learn in order to prepare students to serve well in the contemporary world? What do I need to know about environmental stewardship? The word "ecological" was not even an operating concept back in my college days. Can a responsible person be ignorant about this? Can our education leave it out? What are the implications of our aging population? Does it make a difference to the study of psychology? Of public education? Of nursing? Of politics? Of literature and film studies? Of economics?

c. We should give priority to learning that connects. If the paradigm of graduate education is the specialist researcher coming to know more and more about less and less, then the paradigm of the college scholar ought to be a learning that connects. The disciplines are ways of slicing the pie. They are often defined by a method and by a fairly well-delimited boundary. Our institutions are structured along these boundaries: sociologists here, political scientists there, historians in this other place, biologists down the hall, economists across the square, the people who study religion in the basement across the hall from the mathematicians. The message we give ourselves and our students is that these disciplinary distinctions represent a reality which is also neatly divided.

I believe this world picture is a lie. It may have a certain functionality, but it is a gross academic oversimplification. Mark Taylor in his article "End the University as We Know It" proposes that traditional disciplines and departments be replaced by what he calls "problem-focused programs." What would happen if the focus of our study was a topic like "water"? Who would it make sense to bring to the table to understand such a reality? Geologists? Biologists? Economists? Political scientists? Anthropologists? Students of world religions? Communications? Of course, all of these plus others would make sense. The topic shows the artificiality of the academically divided world and the relative poverty of the world view that it spawns. Here are a few more foci to consider: land, the city, the nation-state, religion, ethnicity, knowledge.

A good friend of mine who has a Ph.D. in psychology and who has been for many years a campus pastor recently went back to university to pursue a degree in water resource management. What a valuable scholar! The problem is that his learning and experience make him a misfit for any traditional academic department. But this is, I believe, an indictment of our system of disciplinary departments, not a judgment of him and the scholarly paradigm he embodies.

I have a friend who lacks a Ph.D. in anything but now has three masters degrees: economics, political science, and theology. She cannot be a tenure-track professor because she lacks "the terminal degree," but, fortunately, she has found an institution that values her breadth and connecting mind and has been willing to employ her with several three-year contracts. What do we presume when we suppose that the Ph.D. is more valuable, that it better suits someone to be a good faculty member and a productive scholar in our community? I think this is a presumption we should challenge.

There are other dimensions of culture that could have been discussed—for example, dimensions having to do with the commitment that faculty make to the institution and the commitments that an institution makes to faculty; dimensions having to do with the appropriate or inappropriate use of the word "family" to apply to a college community; dimensions that have to do with trust, power, and the ways that problems are addressed, solved, or avoided; and dimensions addressing racism, sexism, and other forms of abuse. All of these are worthy of discussion, but they are more than I can address here.

My daughter was surely right, the culture of an educational institution is one of the most important things about it and one that cannot completely be discovered without a fairly long visit. Culture is also a thing which changes, and sometimes those changes can be intentional, an effort to make a place better, more effective, and more in line with its basic identity and values.

CHAPTER TWELVE

Six Lutheran Ideas That Would Transform Education

1. Creation and the Stewardship of Creation

The universe in all its amazing detail is God's self-expressive creation, and we are part of it. As Luther put it, "How dare we not know what can be known?" Humans do not own the world; it belongs to God. But humans are uniquely called to be appreciators and stewards of it. Wonder, awe, thanksgiving, and stewardship should shape the way we learn about the world. Think how different that is from a learning that aims at possession, consumption, and control—which seem to be the main values of science and technology in the modern age.

2. Sin and Idolatry

Sin is probably the most misunderstood term in the Christian vocabulary. We often use it to describe what *they* do or have done, that *we* would not think of doing. But Luther made it completely clear that sin is not a moral category; it is an ontological category. It describes how we (all of us) *are*, not what we have or have not done. What we do is, at most, a symptom of how we are. Sin describes how we *are* as humans in relation to God and how we *are* in relation to the world. Sin is our alienation, our blindness, our narcissism, our self-justification, our attempts to be masters, our denial of our creatureliness. All of these are manifestations of sin.

We humans are neither wise enough, nor good enough to be masters of the universe. Even our great ideologies for reforming and controlling the human condition have produced nightmares of destructiveness. We should know this about ourselves and name the gods we are tempted to worship, particularly in the contemporary world: wealth and consumption, nationalism, racism and other chauvinisms, power and destructiveness, oblivion. Each of these names a divinity in the contemporary pantheon, a divinity worshiped by millions in our culture.

What happens if we learn and teach with such awareness in mind? How critical do we need to be? How self-critical? How suspicious of our own isms?

3. Grace and Freedom

God's love is the free gift that liberates us. It is not owed to us, and it certainly is not earned by us. God's saving act liberates us from the power of every attempt to control us and enslave us. It also empowers us to love others. Like a prism, once the pure light of God strikes us, we refract that light/love into a whole spectrum of service to the world.

Luther states, "The Christian is the perfectly free lord of all, subject to none." This implies that we are perfectly free to consider any idea, to read any text, to hear any point of view. We are also freed from the hierarchies established by the culture and from the ultimacies that others thrust on us.

4. Love and Vocation

Luther's discussion of freedom continues: "A Christian is a perfectly dutiful servant of all subject to all . . . Freed from the vain attempt to justify himself [the Christian] should be guided by this thought alone . . . considering nothing but the need of the neighbor."

That refracted love of God is expressed in every station and task that serves the needs of the world: in parenting, in farming, in making shoes, in making good laws, in nursing the sick, in teaching and learning, in making good music.

A college that takes vocation seriously will be self-critical about how it educates professionals. Does the education system serve well the needs of those who come to it in most need? Does the legal system serve the ends of justice and good order, or does it serve the ends of increased litigation and lawyer's fees? Do our health institutions serve well the needs of those in dire need? Do we become healthy in proportion to our use of them?

A college that takes vocation seriously will be concerned that its graduates leave with more than a career. They should also have a calling. They should be more than skilled; they should be caring and concerned. They should have more than a job; they should have an understanding of means, ends, and the dangers that occur when they are confused.

5. The Priesthood of All Believers and *Gottesdienst*

Luther writes:

> When a maid milks the cows or a farmer hoes the field, they serve God more truly than all the monks and nuns. . . . If this could be impressed on common people every servant and every householder would dance for joy and praise God. . . . If everyone regarded their service to the neighbor as service to God the whole world would be filled with *Gottesdienst* [literally 'God service' but also the German term for the worship service].

Luther argued that all work is vocation, that all persons are priests, and that all work is God's work and is, thereby, an act of worship. This means that the distinction many of us are tempted to make—the distinction between the religious and the secular, the sacred and the ordinary, the godly and the worldly—are challenged. How, then, do we study accounting, management, biology, nursing, history, communications, or law? How, for that matter, do we study religion?

6. Loving, Engaged Criticism

Luther was critical. He criticized the church, he criticized the tradition, he criticized the princes, he criticized the common folk, he criticized his fellow theologians, and he certainly criticized himself. While doing that he did not always follow his own advice and "put the most charitable construction on all that he [the neighbor] does."

Luther's criticism was neither skeptical (aimed at believing nothing) nor cynical (aimed at dissociating himself from everything). His criticism was engaged and loving. He was critical because he was deeply engaged, deeply concerned, and deeply in love.

A Lutheran college/university should practice such criticism and self-criticism. That it be an engaged community of discourse should be one of its identifying characteristics.

Afterword

These ideas are not exclusively Lutheran. Luther certainly did not intend that any of them should be taken that way. All are Christian. Some we would expect to be shared by any who take the Bible seriously. Some of them are shared by people of other religions or people who are not religious at all. That makes no difference. They are all ideas that Lutherans, because of their history or theology, have good reason to take seriously. They are all ideas that, if taken seriously, would be able to transform the ends and means of higher education.

I do not think the world needs more generic colleges and universities. I believe that the world desperately needs places that are called by love to be free, critical, and vocational in the ways sketched here.

CHAPTER THIRTEEN

Colleges, Universities, and the Church

Thinking about "Church"

When we begin to think about the relation of colleges and universities to the church we often work with some questionable assumptions:

Assumption 1: Assumptions about "the church"

We are quick to assume that "church" designates some kind of identifiable institution or structure properly denominated. But what if we thought of church as a verb? What if we were to say, "Church is what happens when . . ."?

On hot days in the summer I used to tease my kids by trying to get them to run through the sprinkler to see the back side of the rainbow. For a while they were curious about why the rainbow always disappeared when they went to look for its back side—but not any more; they are now too sophisticated to run through the sprinkler or to be intrigued by such wonders or the stupidity of their father. When I asked my daughter to explain the disappearance of the rainbow, she said, "You can't see it because it's not there." I think there is some wisdom in what she says. But only some.

What if we think of the church as analogous to a rainbow? The church is the diffraction (by means of human community) of the love of God into the world. The church is what happens when the love of God in Christ shines through us. Or as I have written elsewhere, "Church is a living manifestation (in the lives of people) of the love of God for the world, God's embrace that takes the form of the cross."

One thing I like about the rainbow image of church is that it is a metaphor that avoids the either/or we get into about justification, sanctification, passivity, and empowerment. The empowering source is the light, the love of God, without which nothing happens, but the manifestation is in the life of the faithful (those in whom Christ is alive) serving in love the needs of the neighbor.

Assumption 2: That the church needs service vs. the church as service

In his lectures on Genesis about *Gottesdienst* that I quoted in the previous section, Luther explains that *Gottesdienst* is the service of the needs of the neighbor, the needs of the world at hand. It is the way God uses us to care for the world: caring for children, milking the cows, making shoes, cleaning the street, making just laws, teaching students, studying our lessons, washing the dishes again. Luther's parishioners must have asked him, "But shouldn't we be doing something religious? A pilgrimage? A penance? A saint's day celebrated? Some work in or for the church?" Luther's response is that we serve God by serving the needs of the world at hand. That is an act of worship, no matter how ordinary, messy, or earthy it may seem.

A few years ago I visited Lutherans in Australia as a guest of Lutheran Education Australia. I got to see the great success and variety of Lutheran schools there and met with principals, professors, teachers, and social service workers by the hundreds. I discovered something interesting: The Lutheran church (measured in terms of congregations started and members recruited) is fairly static. It is neither growing nor shrinking. On a graph it is basically a flat line. In terms of their theological agreement (e.g., women's ordination) they are quite fractured, strongly disagreeing about some pretty basic things. But the church (measured in terms of its mission—schools started, education programs sponsored, social service programs initiated and supported, people being served) is exploding! For example, the number of K-12 students served in Lutheran schools has sextupled in the last twenty-five years! If we regard the church in terms of its mission, it has a growth curve that goes right off the page. Doing this means that we are in the position of having to count church as the activities of a whole lot of people who are not even Lutheran, because church members obviously cannot do all the activities by themselves. What do we do with such an idea? My suggestion, and I believe Luther's as well, is to call it church.

Assumption 3: Church there, colleges and universities here

The assumption here seems to be that learning, thinking, and teaching (the primary activities of academics) is not itself church. But what (returning to our prism or rainbow analogy) if learning and teaching are ways in which the love of God is refracted into the world? Is teaching a vocation? As such is it a service of the deep needs of the world? It should be. Is it a service of the real needs of our students? Is it not, therefore, *Gottesdienst*?

Or do we want to go back to the idea that the real work of the church is the preaching of the word and the administration of the sacrament? If so, then the closest I will get to *Gottesdienst* is to be a lector at the Sunday worship or hang around to wash communion glassware at the end.

How the University Serves

Besides being a service to our students and to the world by means of our students, the university can also be a service to the wider church.

1. The college/university reminds us that the church has a calling in education. That is, that education is one of the legitimate vocations of the church in the world. The university is one of the hues of the rainbow whereby God's love, diffracted, illumines the world.

2. The university is a place where mission and identity are held in creative tension. Universities are no longer only "by Lutherans for Lutherans." They are places where the Lutheran calling in education reaches out into the whole world. The principle is thereby illustrated that we find ourselves by sharing ourselves with others, not by worrying about the Lutheran difference.

3. The college is a place where both the theory and practice of Christian life-patterns such as earth stewardship, peace making, justice, celebration of difference, community of critical discourse, and growth toward whole humanness can be developed.

4. The university is a place of critical openness and freedom, where the world's ultimacies, values, and chauvinisms can be challenged. It is a place where theology of the cross can be practiced.

5. The university reminds us that love needs to be educated for service and leadership, and it reminds us of the ways that learning may be related to personal growth and transformation.

6. The college/university is the church in the world—or at least a very important part of it. It is this without being very churchy. (Please forgive the equivocation.) A colleague of mine commented about Capital University: "One of the things I like about this place is that it's not very churchy." I responded, "Yes, that's because it's Lutheran."

CHAPTER FOURTEEN

Pounding Nails

About a dozen years ago I was putting in some summer volunteer time working for Habitat for Humanity. Another fellow and I had spent a couple of hours nailing OSB boards on the rafters of a house. We took a break for coffee, and he shared with me that he had connected to Habitat through a Buddhist community in Columbus. I told him that I had connected through a Lutheran church. He said, "A Lutheran, eh? Then your nails can't possibly be going in straight." I laughed out loud. I could see by the twinkle in his eye that he had made the comment with a dose of irony. But I could also tell that there was something a bit serious about what he said. We started talking, and he revealed to me that someone had said the equivalent to him when he had applied to be a middle school math teacher in a Christian school in Cincinnati. They had told him that they gave priority to Christian applicants because they made better teachers even of subjects like middle school math. When he pressed for an explanation the principal had said, "With Christian teachers the love of God comes through and the math comes out right."

Our conversation about this continued for several days as we pounded nails, acquired blisters, extricated slivers, and shared coffee and bagels contributed by a neighborhood deli. The thoughts triggered by that encounter have stayed with me over many years. They linger largely because I have maintained an inner dialogue about the questions that the rooftop encounter initiated. There are three dominant voices of that dialogue:

1. I do not know who the principal was, nor do I know what Christian denomination he represented. My temptation is to imagine him as stupid and narrow, but if I am charitable I can also imagine him saying something like this: Were I hiring someone as a carpenter, my main and perhaps only concern would be, Does he have the skills and experience necessary to do that job? In such a case whether the person

is Christian, Hindu, Buddhist, or atheist makes little difference. That's partly because the job is defined in quite a narrow and one-dimensional way. Can the person use a saw? Can he measure with sufficient accuracy? Can he install drywall? Can he repair a broken door? Those are the relevant questions.

Teaching, on the other hand, is neither a narrow nor a one-dimensional task. It is, in its very nature, relational, bringing into dialogue at least three different things: the student (and the student's gifts and needs), the subject or discipline being taught, and the person of the teacher. Who the teacher is, what the teacher's outlook and values are, and what the teacher believes and is motivated by—all become relevant. What one does and how one does it can be influenced, sometimes strongly, by why one is doing it. Religious beliefs do and should shape values and motivations, and that is why they are relevant to the hiring of teachers, particularly if they are to be teachers in schools that care about the overall growth and development of the student.

I do not think there is anything like Christian chemistry or Christian algebra that I would want to see taught in our school. Chemistry and algebra are two examples of subjects which, if taught well, should be taught in pretty much the same way anywhere. It is not a Christian version of those subjects that I am concerned to see taught. But in the teaching of any subject, values and beliefs are communicated. How do we regard nature? Why should one care about learning math and learning it well? What assumptions about human worth, human relations, and our relationship to nature get communicated by the teacher in the way he regards his subject, relates to the students, and exhibits passion for his subject?

I do not think that Christian teachers of any subject are necessarily smarter or wiser than non-Christians. But I do think that Christian belief may inoculate a person against vulnerability to certain ways of thinking that become popular in the culture. A few decades ago behaviorism was the reigning paradigm of explanation in psychology. Before that the fad seemed to be Freudian analyses and explanations. Christians who were studying and teaching psychology had good reasons to be skeptical and suspicious of both of these theories. They may well have learned them and taught them, but they had good reason to question their adequacy and good reason to critique them for the kind of disciplinary reductionism that they practiced. That does not mean that Christians all need to subscribe to some kind of Christian psychology. They should be excellent inquirers in their field and accept those theories that they find most adequate. But what they are likely to find adequate may be different. Christian belief includes a view of what it means to be a whole person and that, in turn, will influence the theories a psychologist can find acceptable.

I admit that mathematics may be the hardest example to justify with this latter argument. But I do think a case can be made for saying that religious beliefs are not irrelevant in the hiring of teachers and that they are very relevant in the hiring of teachers in many disciplines. None of this is to argue that Christian belief ought to trump every other consideration. Teachers should have a knowledge of and passion for their subjects, and they should have a gift for communicating with the kind of students they will have. Given the importance of those things, other concerns can legitimately be brought to the table.

2. The second voice is one I have used myself, though not very consistently. It is also the voice of many of my university colleagues. Some of them may recognize their contributions to it.

Religious identification or membership should never be used as a criterion for the hiring or promotion of teachers. There are basically three reasons why:

a. Scholarship and teaching owe their allegiance to the service of truth. History shows us many examples where persons who were pursuing truth were silenced or persecuted because they were not conforming to the party line. In many cases the party line has been religiously defined. In some cases it has been politically defined or ideologically defined. The persecution of Giordano Bruno, the trial of Galileo, the horrors of the Inquisition, the persecutions of thinkers in Hitler's Germany, Stalin's Soviet empire, Mao Tse Tung's regime—all of these placed conforming to the party line above the service of the truth and all with absolutely disastrous results.

It would be a mistake, of course, to blame religion for all these examples. We all know of cases where new hires were expected to conform to whatever "school" or academic orthodoxy was being promoted at the time. But religious conformity is an example, like the others, of this horrible mistake. Loyalty and service to the truth should be the only loyalty test that any academic institution ever uses.

b. Some might argue that a devotion to a particular religious view implies a commitment to the truth. But there is ample evidence of instances where that has not been the case. The trial of Galileo is certainly an example of this. It combined a rejection of a particular theory with an unwillingness to do the experiments and the observations that would have been useful in settling the issue. Contemporary religious communities do pretty much the same thing when they reject evolutionary theory or evidences regarding the age of the earth or the cosmos. The "religionists" want to settle the argument with citations from Scripture rather than do the inquiries that are necessary to confirm or falsify hypotheses and theories. There is not good evidence that religious communities are good protectors of the truth. There is better evidence, I think, that open and critical academic communities are good protectors of the truth.

c. What characteristics are supposed to accompany someone's being a Christian, Buddhist, or Muslim? If the argument is made that it is useful to hire Christian or Buddhist teachers because they have compassion, then make compassion the hiring criterion, not Christianity or Buddhism. If the argument is made that Native Americans should be hired because their religion embodies respect for the earth, then make respect for the earth the hiring criterion, not participation in a Native American religion.

Not all people who call themselves by the same religious name share the same values. Some Christians are pacifists, some are chauvinists, many are quite belligerent. So it is doubtful whether any dependable characteristics come with membership in a religious group. Much better would be to describe the characteristics desired and hire where they are found, leaving religious identification in the background, or better, out of the picture altogether.

3. The third voice in some ways builds on the third reason considered above, but with a slight change of view. It is also an outlook that I have heard myself voicing. Some of the metaphors are found elsewhere in this book. It is also a view I frequently hear from colleagues. Part of its attractiveness is that it can be seen as a kind of pragmatic compromise.

It does not matter how our motivations differ, provided that we can all join in the task at hand. The Habitat building project is a good illustration of that. People may have come there for a great variety of reasons including religious ones. Those reasons are not really important, provided that they work cooperatively to get the house built. Talking constantly about whether we are there because of Jesus, the Buddha, or Karl Marx will simply drive us apart. Instead we should focus on what we have in common, not what makes us different. The same thing could apply to a project in education. If we are united about what students should learn and what the best way is to help them learn it, then we can work together to enable and empower their learning. That is where the focus ought to be.

Within a religious tradition the *mythos*, or informing story, of the tradition shapes the belief system. The beliefs, in turn, shape the religious practice of the community. That intra-community practice in turn informs a set of values which inform how we act in the world. The values we hold and the way we act in the world may be identical to the values and actions of other groups, informed by different informing stories and different religious practices. If we focus attention on the informing stories or theology, we may find ourselves in deep disagreement. If we focus on values, actions, and needs of the neighbor, we find ourselves united in action and effort. Isn't that what Luther recommends when he says: "Freed from the vain attempt to justify himself [the Christian] should be guided by this thought alone . . . considering nothing but the need of the neighbor."

I may do volunteer work on several environmental protection efforts because I believe the Bible makes clear that we are called by God to serve as stewards of the creation. If I constantly talk about God, the Bible, and my call as a steward, I may find myself alienated from those who care about nature for very different reasons. But why focus the attention there? A school, whether a university or elementary school, requires a lot of people working together. If they can work cooperatively, wonderful. If they espouse the same values, that is wonderful too, for it makes the chance of successful, cooperative effort so much the greater. But if we insist that they also share our theology, religious practices, and informing story—well, good luck.

The religious heritage of a school should be like the roots of a tree, nourishing the visible parts of the tree and finally producing fruit.

We would not want to cut the trunk or branches off from the root. Nor would we want to plant the tree upside down and have the roots waving around in the open air. They belong out of sight, perhaps the deeper the better.

There are some things I like about each of these views. I think each points to something important, and I think it would be a shame if any of the three voices were silenced. If I could count on someone voicing the other two, I would be happy to become known for arguing only one. But so far I am stuck carrying on this debate with myself.

CHAPTER FIFTEEN

Temptations and Trees Without Roots

Major Temptations

I think there are three major dangers for colleges and universities like ours in the contemporary world. They are dangers because they are temptations, and they are temptations because they appeal to something deep in our nature. We fall for them over and over again:

1. There is the temptation of religious insularity, moving back toward what I called the for us/by us model of religious education and religious identity. We are clearly *us* if we can easily see how we are not like *them*.

2. There is the temptation of becoming generic institutions delivering generic courses toward generic degrees in a perfectly transferable marketplace. We want to become just like them.

3. There is the temptation of becoming elite colleges hosting elite students funded by elite parents and supported by elite alumni and federal research grants. This latter one may not be a temptation for all of us because it is so far beyond our realization, but I think the danger lies not only in achieving such things but also in being tempted by them.

I have seen institutions hover between the first two for decades, assuming that they had to go down one of those two roads. What is required is sufficient insight or chutzpa to challenge that assumption.

Temptations that Accompany the Vocation Model

In an earlier section (Chapter 5) I talked about two models for Lutheran higher education. Each of these models has its own temptations. Here I want to focus on three temptations that may arise for institutions following the vocation model:

1. The temptation to let the secular economy define vocation, namely as training for a market defined job in market defined institutions is a risk. We all do this to an extent. We train nurses and teachers for certification; we educate law and accounting students to pass their licensure exams, etc. But part of educating for vocation also entails using that notion as a critical tool asking: "How well do our professions and our institutions serve the needs of those in society who need them most? So we are interested in knowing what percentage of our law school graduates pass the bar exam, but we are also interested in knowing what kind of attorneys they become. Are the needs of the needy thereby served? Is the cause of justice well-advanced? Or does the profession of attorney primarily serve the end of increased litigation and the needs of the attorneys?

2. The temptation to offer generic education, i.e. a consumption of courses and programs that are easily and immediately replaceable, transferable, and outsourceable. Once again to a certain extent this is unavoidable and not bad. I expect that what students learn in my logic course will be very much like what they would learn in a beginning logic course at Ohio State or at Columbus State for that matter. The problem is not that this ever occurs. The problem is that it becomes the norm for education at our institutions.

If we tell ourselves, our students, and their parents that what they are getting are generic courses as part of a generic curriculum offered by generic teachers, then the very next question they are going to ask is, "Why shouldn't I buy these courses at the cheapest price possible?" "Why shouldn't I get the best of all worlds, a Columbus State education and a Capital University degree?"

I believe that this perception is why we, at Capital University, have a fairly high attrition rate. It is not because we do not have good teachers. It is not because we are not nice to our students. It is because we have not bothered to explain to them while we had them what difference an education informed by the Lutheran tradition makes. We have not communicated our mission, our calling. We have not told our story. We have not explained why we have the curriculum we do, require the studies we do, teach the way that we do, have the critical edge that we do.

Many of us finally fall for the generic education model on the assumption that "the market" demands that we become generic institutions. What academic leaders fail to realize is that if you are going to play the generic institution game, you have to sell cheap in order to compete with the Walmarts of the academic world. Few of us can sell cheap enough to do that. The other consequence of providing a generic education is that you graduate a whole generation of alumni who have no more loyalty to your college than they do to the grocery store where they shop for the best deal on toilet paper. My prediction is that if we try to play the generic education game, we will lose, and no one will mourn our passing.

3. The temptation to forget that the tree of which we are part has a Lutheran trunk and Christian roots. I often begin my Introduction to Philosophy class by asking some student to come up to the board and draw a tree. (Because philosophy is a *radical* discipline, it digs around at the roots.) The student will draw a pretty tree—leaves, branches, trunk, sometimes even fruit. But every time they do this they forget the roots—understandably so, because the roots are the part we do not ordinarily see. Most of the time when we look at the tree of education we pay attention to the branches (of knowledge). We want to know what someone is majoring in. That is, we want to know the branch in which they are nesting. Once in a while when we have discussions about general education, we take note of the trunk (though most academicians believe that stuff cannot possibly be as important as what is taking place out on my branch). Infrequently we take note that the tree also has roots. Yet, following the metaphor, we know full well that the tree cannot be healthy if it does not have roots or if the branches have severed their connection to them.

When we are tempted to become generic institutions offering generic courses in generic curricula, we easily become involved in this severing of roots. An education made up of generic courses is a bundle of branches without roots. If we do not connect our thinking about curriculum to our roots, if we do not connect the way we structure and prioritize learning for our students to our institutional story and mission, then we cannot be surprised that students do not see the connection.

The Nurture of Trees

How do we connect branches to roots? Whose job should it be to remind us of this connection? Whose job should it be to ask perennially and pervasively, "Why we do this?" The best answer to this "who" question is to say that it is primarily the job of the president and the board of trustees. The president ought to be able to explain to anyone who asks how the branches of the tree are connected to the trunk and how the trunk is connected to the Christian and Lutheran roots of the whole enterprise. I think a large number of the trustees should be able to do this as well. This does not mean that the president must be a professional theologian or a former professor of Reformation studies. It does mean that the president should be able to understand enough about the tradition to see the essential connections between roots, trunk, and branches. I said this is the best answer, but of course it is not the most realistic answer. As a matter of fact, many of our presidents do not feel at all comfortable doing this and wish to avoid historical or theological discussions whenever possible.

So, what else might work? In some places the task of reminding the college of its theological roots falls to a diminishing number of faculty. That may work, provided that those faculty are respected and heard. But it only works as long as those faculty are there. What happens when they retire or die? Who, then, becomes the bearer of the Lutheran concern and the asker of the root-connected question?

The problem with putting the responsibility in the hands of the president or some particular faculty is that it is then so contingent on those people being there and being people who have an interest and an ability to carry out this task. What if we institutionalize this task, building it into the structure of the place in some way that cannot be easily avoided? This could happen in different ways:

1. By establishing a chair whose holder is required to converse with fellow faculty and administration about root-connectedness

2. By establishing a center, the function of which is to sponsor occasions for such dialogue

3. By establishing an annual day or week of faith and learning where the community gathers to hear a speaker or group and carry on such conversations

4. By sponsoring an annual retreat for a rotating twelve to fifteen staff and faculty focused on such conversation

5. By offering an annual short course retreat for the theological education and refreshment of ELCA presidents, board chairs, and campus leaders.

Strategic Questions

1. Will announcing our roots too loudly, too clearly, drive away prospective students, parents, and faculty who are not of that persuasion? The function of roots, after all, is to remain underground.

2. Will focusing on education for service in a way that non-Lutherans and non-Christians can be a part drive away those who are looking for an explicitly Christian or Lutheran education?

3. Some have suggested a structure like this: *Story* informs *theology* informs *values* informs *practice.* While we tell our story and expound our theology in the presence of fellow Lutherans, in public why do we talk only about values and practice? Is that the strategy our institutions should embody?

4. Are there better and worse ways of encouraging and enabling the dialogue necessary to maintain a connection of branches to roots? Consider these alternatives:

- The "now we're going to teach you something Lutheran" approach.

- "Here's a foundational question and here are some answers, at least one of which is essentially Christian/Lutheran. What do you think of it?"

- "Can we learn anything useful from our Christian/Lutheran heritage that will help us discover good answers to our vital questions?"

5. Are there ways of speaking about our roots that are exclusive and alienating? Are there ways of speaking about them that are inclusive and inviting?

6. Should we expect that the answers to these questions will be the same everywhere or always be the same at the same institution?

I do not think there is a single set of right answers to these questions, but I believe the questions themselves are important and informing. They should be kept alive, as should the concerns they embody.

CHAPTER SIXTEEN

Some Things I Just Do Not Understand

More times than I want to remember I have heard otherwise intelligent people say, "We shouldn't be an obviously Christian or Lutheran college because we don't want to offend non-Christians." This response must be deeply embedded in the culture somewhere, because it is so often repeated as though the truth of it were obvious.

Maybe I am an odd duck or a truly unusual person (my kids and colleagues nod in agreement), but I have never been "offended by" someone else's religious viewpoint or expression. Many years ago I interviewed for a position at a Catholic (Benedictine) university. It never occurred to me to be offended by their on-campus church, their religion requirements, or the visual presence of the community of monks. I have been in Jewish communities, Hindu communities, Buddhist communities, and Native American communities. In each of these cases, I was there as an outsider, as a minority, and in some cases as an ignorant observer. In none of those cases did I ever feel offended. In all of my travels to Lutheran conferences and campuses I have met many faculty and staff of Lutheran colleges and universities who were not Lutheran, not Christian, or not religious at all. I have never heard anyone say that they felt excluded, alienated, or second-class to Lutheran faculty and staff because they themselves were not Lutheran. In fact I know only one story of a person who was made to feel very unwelcome at a Lutheran college, and he was a Lutheran and a noted Lutheran theologian as well.

None of this is to deny that Christians have treated non-Christians badly. We have. It is not to deny that Christians have treated each other badly. That is true, too. Maybe the assumed offense is a remnant of the Inquisition, the religious wars, the pogroms, and the persecutions that are too prevalent in our history. For all these things we must earnestly repent and ask forgiveness.

I understand the hurt that people may feel around a group that has persecuted or harmed them. As an American I could feel that way about the Japanese, the Germans, or people of the Muslim faith. I am part Native American, so I suppose I could hate the Europeans who so badly treated my ancestors. My problem, though, is that some of those European perpetrators were also my ancestors. So while I could condemn the actions of particular groups, nations, or generations, I know that I finally cannot maintain such a view. I cannot blame or fear contemporary Germans, Japanese, or Muslims because of what was done by their ancestors or some members of their community. To do so would be both unjust and irrational. The continuation of resentment and hatred is what fuels centuries-long feuds and wars, national, ethnic, racial, and religious. What George W. Bush called "the axis of evil" runs through our own hearts.

As I say, I just do not understand the idea that someone would be offended by the explicit religiousness of a college or university. If someone can make this clear to me, I will be grateful. The Lutherans I hang out with are a very open and accepting community. They not only tolerate difference, they value it. If at some time in the future they quit doing so, I will be offended, not by their being Christian or being Lutheran, but by their having fallen for one or another form of chauvinism. Let us be a welcoming place *because* we are Christian.

CHAPTER SEVENTEEN

Two Ways to Ruin a University

Of course there are more than just two ways to ruin a university. For focus and dramatic effect I want to consider just two for now and repent of it later. The two I select happen to be analogous to two stories that ran on the TV news The one story was about the collapse of a family business that occurred because of inattention to finances, mounting debt, and gross cost over-runs. The other was about the murder-suicide of a billionaire and his wife, despondent at having just lost a million dollars in the marketplace. Both of these tragedies occurred because of inattention. The one was inattention to the numbers. The second occurred because someone mistook their life for a set of numbers.

Failure by Mismanagement

Mismanagement is a process of losing track of the economics of what one is doing. One can lose track of profits and expenses; one can make investments one cannot afford; one can misunderstand or misguess the marketplace, misestimate income, or fail to foresee or count the full costs. Mismanagement occurs when decision making is not informed by accurate accounting. This can occur if our accountants do not know what they are doing, if they do not care, or if they are silenced by decision makers. We are all familiar with such cases, and we are probably all familiar with the consequences of mismanagement.

Failure by Management

If mismanagement is bad then isn't management bound to be good? Not necessarily. We usually do not have any trouble identifying mismanagement, particularly after the fact. But my guess is that we are not so able to identify the ruinous character of management. That is why more needs to be said about it.

If mismanagement is the lack of connection between effective accounting and decision making, ruinous management is *when accounting takes the place of decision making.* Someone once said, "Economics makes a wonderful servant, but it makes a horrible master." A university may be organized to do a wonderful job of accounting, collecting and communicating data: students admitted, tuition discounting rates, costs of running the admissions office, costs of student affairs programming, calculation of FTE faculty teaching loads, enrollment and retention profiles, profits and costs by major, programs, etc. All of these data are necessary for good decision making in a university. The problem occurs when the collection and recitation of such data becomes decision making.

I would say that a university that makes its decisions solely by counting hours or dollars is a place that has lost its vision and sense of mission and identity. It is no longer a place aimed at doing something good and important in the world. It is admitting in a sense, "We don't any longer know what we're doing or why we're doing it, but we know exactly how much we've made or lost in the process." It has replaced a vision of education with a vision of schooling units sold. It has replaced the vision of transforming and enabling the growth of persons with the vision of processing customers. Its vision of faculty is no longer valued persons in a community, but the labor half of the labor/management world. Increasingly it is labor that is out-sourced. The motto engraved in the lintel of Old Main may still read *"Veritas," "Sapientia Omnia Vincit,"* or "Ask, Learn, Serve," but it often really means "Generic products sold cheap here" or "Whatever." Jesus long ago offered a warning about such transformation of economic vision when he posed the question: "What does it profit a man to gain the whole world and lose his soul?" The sarcastic answer is, of course, "a world of profit." Exactly the same question can be asked about a university and, again, the point of the question may be missed by those who most need to hear it.

There is a time to lament the financial ruination of a university. It is easy to tell when that occurs because the sheriff (or other authority) shows up to take possession of the property and sells it off to cover the debts. But there is also a time to mourn the loss of the soul of a university. There the death is not so obvious. Like hospital patients whose heartbeat, breathing, and passage of fluids between bags is closely measured and monitored, many institutions survive from one accounting cycle to the next. Once in a while somebody may stop to reflect about them, "I wonder who they were?" and, "Does anybody still care?"

Works Cited

Adams, E.M. *A Society Fit for Human Beings* (Albany, New York: SUNY Press, 1997).

Berry, Wendell. "Christianity and the Survival of Creation," *Sex, Economy, Freedom and Community* (New York: Pantheon, 1993).

Bloom, Benjamin, et al. *Taxonomy of Educational Objectives: Handbook I, The Cognitive Domain* (Chicago: Longmans, 1956).

Christenson, Tom. *The Gift and Task of Lutheran Higher Education* (Minneapolis: Fortress Press, 2003).

Dalos Parks, Sharon. *Big Questions, Worthy Dreams* (San Francisco: Jossey Bass, 2000).

Gellner, Ernest. *The Legitimation of Belief* (London: Cambridge University Press, 1974).

Glazer, Steven. "Introduction," *The Heart of Learning: Spirituality in Education.* (New York: Putnam, 2002).

Hi-Ho lyrics from *Snow White and the Seven Dwarfs* (Walt Disney website).

Kohak, Erazim. "Selves, People, Persons," *Boston University Studies in Philosophy and Religion*, Vol. 13 (South Bend, Indiana: University of Notre Dame Press, 1993).

Lessing, Doris. *Prisons We Choose to Live Inside* (New York: Harper and Row, 1987).

Luther, Martin. "Heidelberg Disputations," *Basic Theological Writings*, Timothy Lull, ed. (Minneapolis: Fortress Press, 1989).

"Selections from the Lectures on Genesis," *Basic Theological Writings, op. cit.*

"Letters to the Councilmen of Germany. . . " *Basic Theological Writings, op. cit.*

"On the Freedom of the Christian," *Basic Theological Writings, op. cit.*

Martin, James. *The Meaning of the 21st Century* (New York: Riverhead/ Penguin, 2007).

Merton, Thomas. *Choosing to Love the World* (Boulder, Colorado: Sounds True Press, 2008).

Orr, David. *Earth in Mind: Education, Environment and the Human Prospect* (New York: Island Press, 2004).

Palmer, Parker. *A Hidden Wholeness: The Journey Toward an Undivided Life* (San Francisco: Jossey Bass, 2004).

Reman, Rachel. "Education for Mission, Meaning and Compassion," in Steven Glazer, *The Heart of Learning, op. cit.*

Taylor, Mark C. "End the University As We Know It," *The New York Times*, op-ed section, April 27, 2009.

Tranvik, Mark. "Sinning Boldly on Campus," *The Cresset* (Valparaiso University, Lent 2009).

Wells, H.G. *The First Man in the Moon* (London: Macmillan, 1901).